HANDBOOK OF SMALL BUSINESS ADVERTISING

HANDBOOK OF SMALL BUSINESS ADVERTISING

Michael Anthony
Applied Training Service

ADDISON-WESLEY PUBLISHING COMPANY
Reading, Massachusetts • Menlo Park, California
London • Amsterdam • Don Mills, Ontario • Sydney

Library of Congress Cataloging in Publication Data

Anthony, Michael, 1944-
  Handbook of small business advertising.

  I. Advertising.   2. Small business.   I. Title.
HF5823.A777   659.1   80-14858
ISBN 0-201-00086-5

ISBN-0-201-00086-5
ABCDEFGHIJ-AL-89876543210

ADVERTISING DOESN'T PAY! ... OH??

Why is it when people wake up in the morning after sleeping on an advertised mattress under an advertised blanket and pull off their advertised pajamas . . . take a bath in an advertised tub, brush their teeth with advertised toothpaste, wash with advertised soap, put on advertised clothes, sit down to breakfast consisting of advertised products, drive to the office in an advertised car, write with an advertised pen . . . then refuse to advertise, saying advertising does not pay, and then if business isn't good enough, they advertise their business for sale!

If you believe in your business and want to build it into something to be proud of . . . advertise it!

Author Unknown

ACKNOWLEDGMENTS

For fear of sounding like an Academy Award acceptance speech, I couldn't possibly thank all of those marvelous people who have contributed something of themselves to this book. There are of course some very special people who cannot go without mention.

First, my wife Karen, who at first had no idea what I was doing, but stuck by me anyway.

George Morrisey for his insistence that I offer my knowledge to Addison-Wesley and then helped me agonize over getting everything done right.

Randy Reid, who did his very best to correct years of incorrect spelling and punctuation for me.

And last but not least, Dick Staron of Addison-Wesley, whose friendship and professional dedication to this project made it possible for me to share a little of what I know with many who can use it.

A sincere thank you to all of you and all of the people at Addison-Wesley who worked on this book.

CONTENTS

1
THE PURPOSE OF THIS MANUAL

In the beginning human beings found very simple ways of obtaining the basic commodities needed to sustain life. It was a simple matter to band together and exchange those things necessary for health, comfort, and survival.

As societies expanded and became more complex, the needs of human beings became more sophisticated. Thus, people started looking for more productive, efficient ways of obtaining those things that made life more comfortable. It was found that one member of the tribe or clan could be responsible for providing certain commodities, and other members could provide other commodities. Under this system, each person was able to trade some commodities in order to obtain other commodities needed to make his or her life more comfortable.

As the tribes were transformed into larger organizations, such as cities, states, and countries, it became apparent that many people would have to perform the same task in order to produce sufficient quantities to meet the demand for a particular product or service. Thus was born the world of commerce. Competition among the producers of products and services became the very basis for increased quality and efficiency. Without competition we would have no choice of products. Without competition many of the things that we enjoy today might never have been invented.

As new products and services were introduced, it became necessary to inform people about them. As long as any new product or service remained unknown, it would remain unsold. Thus was born the world of advertising.

In the complex world of today, advertising is one of the key factors in the success of trade. If we were not able to inform the marketplace about the existence and particular qualities of our products and our services, we would not be able to conduct business at all. Matters are additionally complicated because modern society is changing so rapidly that it is very difficult to define what a particular product or service can provide to a given public. Nevertheless, although it is complex in theory, it need not be complex in its application. It has been my observation that anyone who is truly interested in using advertising effectively can do so.

Most people opening a business of their own begin their particular venture because of a desire to be independent, as a quest for personal satisfaction, and, of course, in order to make money. In many cases businesses are born out of a keen interest in some product or field. Some fortunate people have been able to turn interesting and enjoyable hobbies into outstanding business ventures. Others have simply recognized a need in the populace and have set out to fill that need.

Once an individual has decided to enter a particular business or field, he or she must then begin the arduous process of establishing the functioning business. Once individuals actually begin running a business venture, the importance of telling others what they are doing—and what the benefits of their product are for the customer—becomes obvious.

Unfortunately, many individuals do not realize the value of advertising until they have experienced some type of a setback because of a lack of exposure. Many individuals spend years—even decades—saving enough money to found independent businesses. Then, after saving their money and making a lot of hard sacrifices, they finally realize the dream of having a business of their own, only to have it fail. And why do these small business ventures so often fail? Because the owners put their total investment into the physical location and inventory and fail to make allowances for the cost of advertising or for the time it takes for an advertising program to produce the desired results.

Very often new businesspeople will expect success because they have put so much love, money, and time into their new venture and because they have told everyone they know that they are now in business. They expect the doors to open automatically. Other new business owners frequently plan for advertising but do not really understand the way it functions or the results that should be expected.

Advertising in both retail and industrial businesses must be planned and executed in a proper manner if it is to produce the desired results. Planning, organization, and proper execution are of the utmost

2

importance. The purpose of this manual is to help you develop an effective advertising program.

HOW ADVERTISING WORKS

Advertising is the communication of a message through a preselected medium (or media). The purpose of the advertising message is to influence the receivers' actions or thoughts. This sounds like a very simple process. You as the business define what you have to offer; the buyer makes a decision about the offer, then takes action. Unfortunately, as you are probably aware, the message that is received by the customer is frequently different from the message that was sent by the business. Once the human element is introduced into the communication process, the procedure becomes more complex.

Figure 1.1 illustrates some of the elements that must be considered when communicating. On the one hand, there are certain considerations that you as the sender must take into account before sending the message:

► Who is the receiver?

► What is the best medium (or media) to use to reach that receiver?

► What times are the best to reach that receiver?

► Where are the receivers you are trying to reach?

► What do you have that you believe they want?

► What types of products or services can they afford?

► How do you get them to respond to your offer?

FIGURE 1.1

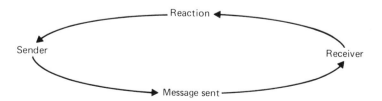

Upon closer examination we find that the actual communication process looks more like that shown in Fig. 1.2.

FIGURE 1.2

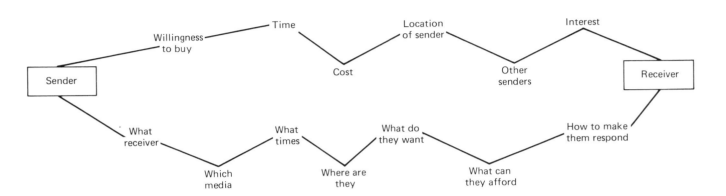

On the other hand, the receiver (customer) has certain decisions to make before your effort to communicate is brought full circle. Is he or she interested in what you have to offer? What do the others offering the same product or service have to offer? Where is the sender located? Is the cost of the product or service affordable? Does the receiver have the time to participate in your business? Is the receiver happy with both product and business and ready to buy?

To be realistic, the true aim of advertising should be to develop sustaining customers who will return time and time again. I call this system the *Customer-Development Process.* Because few of the products we purchase during a lifetime are one-time purchases, it stands to reason—and research has proved—that we tend to buy what has pleased us before, and to buy where we were the most satisfied.

But it is the "American way" to look for better and more efficient methods of obtaining the things we need. Customers are constantly looking for better products and better service. As you can well imagine, there are always competitors trying to lure away your customers. Today your business may be a well-known store with a very large volume of business; tomorrow you may be failing because you did not constantly remind your customers and prospective customers that you are their favorite or could be their favorite store.

How do you keep that constant reminder out in front of the public? Through the constant use of effective advertising! It is not enough to tell your story once. People are fickle and they forget; they must be reminded of what you sell, why they should buy it, and why they should buy it from you. Furthermore, advertising has a very definite cumulative effect. Like a snowball, it picks up new readers, listeners, or viewers every time it's placed before the public.

You should keep in mind that it is much cheaper to hold on to an old customer than to generate a new one, but in order to grow, you must have both. You should also remember that in spite of all you do you will lose some of your old customers. Some will move out of your area, others will change their buying habits, and some will inevitably be attracted to the competition. Young married couples are establishing buying habits; so are students and young workers. These population groups may not now be buyers, but they will be soon. They too must be cultivated. Remember, new customers must be won if you are to hold your ground, and they are imperative if your business is to grow.

2
WHAT IS ADVERTISING AND WHAT DOES IT DO?

What is advertising? Many people have tried to define it. The American Marketing Association has described it as mass, paid communication whose purpose is to "impart information, develop attitudes, and induce favorable action for the advertiser."

This "favorable action" is not necessarily buying. In industrial advertising, it may be listening to a personal sales presentation or simply asking for an estimate. In retail advertising, it may be a visit to the store for a firsthand examination of the merchandise. But to be successful, advertising must bring the advertiser and the potential customer together.

With the exception of mail-order selling, advertising is not expected to close the sale. In later chapters we will get into some specifics as to how the sale is made in response to advertising pull. Most sales are made by personal selling. Even when no personal selling seems to be involved, as in self-service stores, other factors besides advertising usually enter into the decision to buy. Among these are the product itself, the reputation of the maker or of the store where the product is shown, the package, the price, or a point-of-purchase display. It is important to recognize what advertising can and cannot do.

For industrial goods, personal selling carries a greater burden than advertising. This is generally because of the larger sums of money and the technical aspects involved in such purchases. Most of these types of sales may be for large expensive items or on long-term installment contracts.

For consumer goods, personal selling assumes a more important role as prices increase and consumers need more help in making their decisions. When you as a shopper go to the supermarket, there generally is no one there to sell you the items you are shopping for, but when you go to buy an item of a more personal choice, such as a new suit of clothing, or a new car, there is usually a clerk or salesperson there to help influence your decision to buy.

LOOKING AT ADVERTISING AS A DEVELOPMENT PROCESS

As you can see, the theory becomes a test of concise planning, organization, and execution. Each time you as the sender send a message you must keep in mind that the receiver *does not:*

- ► know who you are.

- ► know what your company does.

- ► know where you are.

- ► know what your product does or what your service is.

- ► know what your company stands for.

- ► know what your company's reputation is.

- ► know what you wish to sell.

By addressing these points in your advertising, you will be able to presell your business. Then, making the actual sale will become much easier.

By continually placing this information in front of the public, you will make your company more familiar to the consumer. It is a proven fact that most people shop those businesses with which they are the most familiar and comfortable. Use good advertising to make your business visible and familiar! Also have a plan. See, for example, Table 2.1.

While each individual will be motivated to buy based on his or her own individual need and financial resources, we must concern ourselves here with advertising that is directed toward groups rather than toward the single individual.

Advertising that is directed toward groups may be either *directional* or *intrusive*.

Directional advertising is advertising that tells people *where to buy*. This sort of advertising presumes that the decision to buy (the intent) has already been made. The buyer knows what he or she wants,

19 _____

**TABLE 2.1
Advertising
Distribution Plan**

MEDIA	JAN.	FEB.	MAR.	APR.	MAY	JUNE	JULY	AUG.	SEPT.	OCT.	NOV.	DEC.
Newspaper												
Magazines												
Direct Mail												
Television (local)												
Television (regional)												
Radio (local)												
Radio (regional)												
Direct Response												
Other												

Year To Date Planned_____

Year End Used_____

but either does not know where to get it or wants to investigate several sources before making the purchase.

The classified secton of your telephone directory contains pure directional advertising. Supermarket advertising in newspapers is another example of directional advertising. People need to eat; they need food. They read the advertisements to find out what is being offered, where, at what cost.

Intrusive advertising is advertising that emphasizes *what* to buy rather than where to buy it. It comes to the attention of readers, listeners, or viewers, not because they are looking for the information, but because you—the advertiser—want them to receive it. Radio and television advertising is almost totally intrusive: your radio or television is turned on to provide news or entertainment; the commercials are beyond your control.

Newspaper and magazine advertising varies in the degree of intrusiveness. Readers open some publications with no thought of buying, but the ads capture their attention. Other publications are read not only for information and entertainment, but for the advertising they carry. Most of the advertising carried in business papers is both intrusive and directional.

In intrusive advertising, the skill with which the advertising message is prepared and presented is crucial. The purpose of the ad is to get the reader's or listener's or viewer's attention and stimulate his or her desire to possess the advertised product or service. The ad should produce some favorable action—a purchase or an opportunity to present your product or service in person so as to be in contention for a future purchase.

WHAT HAPPENS WHEN YOU ADVERTISE?

Action in response to advertising may be direct and immediate or indirect and delayed. Most direct response involves items that are purchased often, such as grocery items and some drug and toilet articles. Soon after the advertising appears the sales take place.

You must remember that direct action is not always a sale. You can obtain direct action of various kinds on less frequently purchased items by using coupons, return cards or envelopes, an offer of literature, or a special inducement, perhaps with a time limit. How soon a sale will result depends on how effective and prompt the follow-up is. In many cases, closing the sale requires personal selling.

For products not purchased often or not urgently needed, buyers are likely to wait until a convenient time to act. Or they may be satisfied for the time being with the product they are using but remember your advertising if they decide to make a change later.

STORE-OWNER RESULTS

If you are a store owner, you can expect advertising to accomplish one or more of the following goals:

► Bring people to the store, some for the first time, to see what you have in the way of regular merchandise.

► Attract buyers, some of them regular customers and others new, to examine what you are offering as a special.

9

► Bring in orders by phone or mail.

► Bring in requests for estimates or for sales representatives to call.

► Remind people of the satisfaction they have had from trading with you in the past and let them know that you hope they will continue to patronize your store.

SERVICE-BUSINESS RESULTS

If the service you sell is personal care and needed often, such as hair styling or dry cleaning, you can expect to persuade people to try your service. They may be new to the community, or they may be dissatisfied with the service they are getting elsewhere. Your advertising is an invitation to try your store.

If, on the other hand, the service you sell is one that is needed less often, such as insurance or rental of sickroom equipment, your advertising keeps the public informed about what you can do and what you have available. Someone who needs your type of service will be more likely to think of your place of business than that of a nonadvertiser.

If the service is needed because of an emergency—plumbing repairs, veterinary services, dental care—your advertising could be the reason why a distracted customer calls you instead of someone else. Of course, it may cause people to remember you in less urgent times as well.

MANUFACTURER'S ADVERTISING RESULTS

If you are a manufacturer, you could expect your advertising to bring about the following results:

► Uncover prospects unknown to you and your sales force.

► Bring inquiries that become leads for salespeople to follow up.

► Get appointments for salespeople making cold calls because the prospect recognizes your company name and may already have some interest in your product.

► Keep customers and prospects reminded of your products between sales calls.

10

► Reach unidentified persons who influence buying. A survey made by an industrial magazine revealed that in one plant manufacturing machinery, only 3 of 19 people who took part in buying decisions were reached by salespersons. The other 16 either could not be or were not contacted.

TEN REASONS WHY YOU SHOULD ADVERTISE

1. NEW PROSPECTS.   Twenty percent of all American families will move this year. Some five million people will be married. The market is in constant change as new jobs and new incomes are created. Ironically, even people who are unemployed are seeking new, less expensive places to shop and live.

2. ADVERTISING MUST BE CONTINUOUS.   The National Retail Merchants Association (NRMA) says "mobility and nonloyalty" are rampant. You must promote your product to get former customers to return and to acquire new ones.

3. YOUR COMPETITION ISN'T QUITTING.   There are only so many people in the market at one time. You've got to advertise to get your share, or lose it to the advertisers who do.

4. ADVERTISING IN A TROUBLED ECONOMY GIVES YOU A SHARP ADVANTAGE OVER COMPETITORS WHO CUT BACK OR CANCEL ADVERTISING.   A five-year survey of more than three thousand companies found advertisers who maintained or expanded advertising saw their sales increase an average of 100 percent. Companies that cut advertising averaged sales increases of only 45 percent.

5. ADVERTISING SETS THE RECORD STRAIGHT.   In a troubled economy rumors and bad news travel fast. Advertising corrects gossip and shoots down false reports—in other words, it projects a positive image.

6. CONTINUOUS ADVERTISING STRENGTHENS YOUR IMAGE . . . FOR TODAY AND TOMORROW.   When people who have postponed buying come back to the marketplace you've got a better chance of getting their business if you've maintained a solid, reliable advertising image.

11

7. ADVERTISING WORKS. (BUSINESSES THAT SUCCEED ARE STRONG, CONSISTENT ADVERTISERS). Sears Roebuck, among the most aggressive and successful retailers, is a consistent advertiser. The company invests more than $20 million annually.

8. ADVERTISING IS THE ONLY WAY TO GENERATE STORE TRAFFIC. NRMA tells retailers that bringing in traffic is the first step not only in making a sale, but also in selling additional merchandise. A survey has shown that for every 100 merchandise items that shoppers plan to buy, they make 30 unanticipated purchases.

9. TO MAINTAIN INTERNAL MORALE. When advertising and promotion are cut, salespeople become demoralized. They may believe the store is cutting back or even going out of business.

10. YOUR DOORS ARE OPEN. Salespeople are on the payroll. As long as you are in business, you have overhead expenses. You have got to advertise to generate a steady flow of customers, now . . . and in the future.

WHO SHOULD ADVERTISE?

Every merchant, manufacturer, salesperson, or service person dreams of controlling 100 percent of the available market. While logically that dream can be no more than just that—a dream—any business can reasonably expect to capture its fair share of this market. Regardless of the type of business, product, or service a business deals in, there is some percentage of the market that has not been reached. Even Coca-Cola, the Post Office, the Telephone Company, and Colonel Sanders have competition. In order to capture and maintain their share of the market, they advertise continually.

Invariably, you will come across those companies that would suggest that they have enough business. Granted, that is an enviable position to be in. Nevertheless, being able to maintain that position, and to improve upon the quantity of their customers, requires continual advertising.

Nothing is perfect, and continual refinement requires constant communications. Remember, there are only a certain number of dollars available in your field. You must be prepared to compete for those dollars.

Should you ever question whether good advertising is effective, ask yourself why you call every cola drink a "Coke," or every facial tissue a "Kleenex," or every lip balm "Chap Stick." Think about it! Advertising is your most precious contact.

IMAGE— WHY THINK ABOUT IT?

Anyone who is in business—the small retailer as well as manufacturers and large industrial companies—should be concerned about image. Many times, the amount of business actually done depends on your company's image. You may have what you think is the right merchandise, at the right price, in the right style or specifications, and in the right size, color, quantity, and quality. But in the final analysis, it is the customers' opinion of the price, quality, and service that is important.

Another important factor is the impression customers have of the owner, manager, executives, salespeople or employees, and overall appearance of the company or store. In many cases, when outside salespeople are used, even little things such as business cards and letterheads become very important. Image has become so important that many larger companies have hired public relations or advertising specialists just to work on improving their company image.

We have all formed opinions about companies or stores based on some contact with these organizations. Negative impressions are created by hostile salespeople, unresponsive service personnel, pricing that seems out of line, or merchandise that did not live up to our expectations. After contacts with a company or store, we form an opinion of it, and if the contact was negative we tend to search out other firms with which to do business. Granted, no company or store can completely avoid these types of unfortunate encounters, but making sure they are held to a minimum is of supreme importance.

If you haven't done so recently, take a look at yourself, your company or store, and your employees. Do you like people? Do you want to serve your customers? Are you concerned about helping them get value for their money? Do your employees feel the same? Does the appearance of your company or business reflect your desire to be of assistance? If your answer to these questions—or at least to most of them—is "YES," then your company's image will be greatly enhanced. If you are not sure what the answer is, maybe you should re-examine your company's image.

PRICE POLICY

A store's price line influences the way people think of its other features. A supermarket learned this when it installed carpeting. One effect of the plush floor covering was to create a higher price image. Customers believed that prices had gone up even though they had not.

Nevertheless, it isn't always advantageous for a store to give the impression that it is a "bargain center." A low price policy can sometimes create an unfavorable image. Some customers feel that low price indicates poor quality and refuse to shop where that type of policy is promoted. Other customers like bargain stores. In their minds, the importance of price varies according to type of product, family income, and competitive offerings, to name a few of the considerations.

Customers' opinions about a store's prices are usually created by the store's advertising, displays, merchandising practices (such as stocking national brands), and location. They also rely on their impression of the store's pricing policies rather than on actual knowledge.

Two questions which can be helpful in your image-building effort are:

► What prices do your customers expect to pay, given the type of location for your business?

► Do your customers consider price as important as quality, convenience, dependability, and selection?

MERCHANDISE VARIETY

Your image improves when customers find in your store a product they like but don't find at other stores. Failure to carry certain items may give a retailer's whole line a bad name. Similarly, when customers find in your store or business products they don't like, they become more critical of the rest of your products. The key is knowing the preferences of your customers.

Here are a few suggestions that may help you to identify some areas that help to improve image:

► Eliminate items that give your customers a negative feeling.

► Add new items which may improve your store's image. For example, a medium-priced store might carry selected styles of prestige shoe brands or some other well-known brand names. By so doing, the store may create in

14

the minds of its customers the impression that its other products also have "prestige."

► In merchandise that has a certain style cycle, try to be the first with the new styles.

► You may want to use a good mixture of private brands to encourage customers to think of your business as distinctive and personalized. Keep in mind that the quality of the private brands must be as good as that of the national brands.

SALESPEOPLE AND EMPLOYEES

Salespeople and other employees who are seen by the customers affect the store or company image. Customers form a negative impression if the educational level of a company's personnel appears to be considerably above or below their own. If a store or company appeals primarily to professional or working people, salespeople should dress and speak in such a way as to make those types of customers feel comfortable.

As we all are aware, the first impression is most likely to be a lasting one. The first contact, even though it may be very brief, must make the customer feel at ease and comfortable about his or her decision to shop at your store.

We have all seen employees of stores standing around engaged in conversation. Most people feel uncomfortable interrupting such conversation. Employees must avoid any type of activity that makes the customer feel like a third party. Salespeople must be direct but very polite; they must make each customer feel that as a customer he or she is the most important person in the world. Everyone likes to feel important.

Here are two suggestions that might help improve your salespeople and employees:

► Once you have identified your customers, decide what image your staff should project. Evaluate dress, speech, poise, and general appearance of your personnel. Check from time to time to see that employees create an impression that is consistent with your type of operation.

► Train employees in product knowledge and constructive advice as to product use. This may seem very elementary, but many businesses fail to back good employees with good ongoing training. The result? Complacent workers.

STORE AND
COMPANY
APPEARANCE

What people see as they pass by your store is another important element in your business image. Even people who never enter the store form an impression from its outside appearance. Your store's outside appearance is a form of advertising that says a lot about who you are and what type of atmosphere you offer. The impression you make may be the reason why a lot of people never even give your business a second glance. Take a very critical look and see if the store appearance says something positive about your business.

CHANGING
YOUR IMAGE

An image is a complex creation, and you should not try to change a store or company image without careful thought and planning. If you are dissatisfied with your store or company image, you should ask three very important questions:

1. What kind of image would serve best in the existing market?

2. What type of image does the store or company have now?

3. What changes can be made that will affect both long- and short-term image(s)?

It is important to keep in mind that small stores and companies cannot be all things to all customers. In fact, one of the major competitive advantages of a small business is that it can be different. Many small businesses have built strong enterprises on an image of a particular specialty.

KEEPING
YOUR IMAGE
SHARP

Just like anything else, your store or company image will not stay bright by itself. It requires constant upgrading and maintenance.

Maintaining a store or company image—regardless of the type—can be handled in the same manner as you handle other management problems. Review your image periodically just as you review your financial statements from time to time. Keeping on top of these matters can help you to correct any problems before they get out of hand.

Listen to your customers. Ask them what they like about your store or company and why they prefer it to others of the same kind. Their answers will give you insight into the strong points in your marketing mix and its image. They also will tip you off about what products and services you should be advertising.

All customers "speak" sales. What they buy or don't buy speaks louder than words. Keeping track of sales is one of the best ways of learning what your customers like and don't like.

You should also look at what your competitors are doing. Do some comparative shopping; try to find out what their strong points are and how they are used to create attractive images.

3
MARKETING —
A VITAL
FUNCTION

The term marketing is one that is frequently misunderstood. It has been used to describe the sales function, the advertising plan, and even in some cases the general operating plan of the company. Certainly all of these areas are affected or are actually part of the marketing concept, but they are not the true function of marketing.

WHAT IS MARKETING?

The American Marketing Association describes marketing as "the systematic gathering, recording, and analyzing of data about problems related to the marketing of goods and services."

Marketing research is an organized way of finding objective answers to questions that every successful businessperson must ask:

- ► Who are my customers and potential customers?

- ► What kind of people are they?

- ► Where do they live?

- ► Why do they buy?

- ► Can and will they buy?

- ► Am I offering the kinds of goods and services they want—at the right place, at the best time, and in the right amounts?

- ► Are my promotional programs working?

18

> ► What do customers think of my business?

> ► How does my business compare with competitors?

Listen to noncustomers as well. The people who do not do business with you will frequently turn out to be your best sources of information concerning what is weak in your business image. It is sometimes difficult to get this information, but you may be able to pick up tips from your associates in civic clubs and other community organizations. You might also ask your employees to ask their friends and relatives.

Exchange a check. You can sometimes find another business-person in the same field or a similar field who would agree to come in and check your operations image for you in exchange for your doing the same investigation for his or her business. This other person would have to be from another community so as to avoid issues of competitive conflict. When you check over someone else's business and when you know that someone is checking yours, you become much more aware of those little things that produce a good strong image.

Above all, remember to check your image often. Set objectives that can be met so you'll know when you have accomplished those tasks that will help develop a good company image.

Marketing research is not a perfect science. It deals with people and their constantly changing likes and dislikes. What people want to buy can be affected by hundreds of influences, many of which simply can't be identified. The purpose of marketing research is to study markets scientifically. What this means is trying to gather facts in orderly, objective ways in order to find out how things are, not how you think they are or would like them to be, and what people want to buy, not what you want to sell them.

WHY DO MARKET RESEARCH AT ALL?

Marketing research focuses and organizes business information. It ensures that the information is timely, and it provides what you, the business owner, need to:

> ► Spot problems and potential problems in your current markets.

> ► Reduce business risks.

> ► Identify and profit from sales opportunities.

► Get basic facts about your market to help you make better decisions and set up useful action plans.

HOW TO GO ABOUT MARKET RESEARCH

Defining the problems is the first step. This is so obvious that it is often overlooked. Yet, it is the most important step in the entire process.

You must be able to see beyond the symptoms to get at the cause. Regarding the problems as a "sales decline" is not defining the cause; it is listing a symptom.

In defining your problem, list every possible influence that may have caused it. Has there been a change in the area from which your customers have traditionally been drawn? Have their tastes changed? Have you kept up with the latest trends? List all the possible causes. Then set aside any that you don't think can be measured, since you won't be able to take any action on them.

You must establish an idea of the problem with causes that can be objectively measured and tested. Put your idea of the cause in writing. Look at it frequently while you gather your facts, but don't let your idea get in the way of the facts. Incidentally, you might use the same approach to investigate potential opportunities, too.

Once you have formally defined your problem, you should assess your ability to solve it immediately. If it can be solved directly, then make the necessary adjustments.

What if you're not sure you have enough information at this point to make the proper decision? Here you have to make a subjective judgment to weigh the cost of more information against its usefulness. If you find it necessary to pursue more research, my suggestion is to think cheap and stay close to home. Before considering anything costly, like surveys or field experiments, look at your own records and files. Look at sales records, complaints, receipts, or any other records that can show you where your customers live or work or how and what they buy. Marketing research is limited only by your imagination. Much of it you can do with very little cost except for time and mental effort.

DETERMINING OVERALL OBJECTIVES

We have now determined that marketing research is an important part of our planning stage as well as a vital part of our ongoing business effort. But before we can actually get into the development of our advertising effort, we must establish precise objectives. Keep in mind that if you do not define where you are going, chances are you won't be able to get there.

Once you have established specific measurable goals and objectives, you will have no trouble converting market research into good, usable marketing techniques which will produce good, effective, profitable advertising.

In larger companies, the term "objectives" can encompass a whole management philosophy. This philosophy is generally called Management by Objective, or MBO. In smaller companies, the objective-setting process can be handled in a much more simplified form. Objective planning can be likened to taking a trip:

> ► What do we want to do?

> ► Where do we want to go?

> ► How will we get there?

> ► How much time do we have?

> ► How much money can we spend?

It is immediately apparent that several of these factors are interrelated. The amount of money we have available may affect where we go and how much time we take. The route we take will depend on both time and money.

Let us now concentrate on refining this formula for better planning of your business advertising strategy.

AREAS OF CONCENTRATION

There are seven basic areas we must consider:

1. What we are trying to accomplish with our advertising (ultimate objective).

2. The message content the ads must convey.

3. Current or prospective customers.

4. The media channels of communication.

5. The budget needed to reach the consumer.

6. The time allotted for the campaign.

7. The personnel who will handle the campaign in whole or part.

In a simplified form we can say we must:

1. Determine what the business can offer.

2. Determine who our customers are.

3. Determine where they are located.

4. Determine how best to reach them.

5. Determine how best to motivate them.

IMMEDIATE OBJECTIVES AND GOALS

There are two main objectives to consider when planning objectives and goals for a business:

1. Promote the sale of merchandise or services.

2. Promote the business as a total institution.

No matter how much "sell" you place on the merchandise or service that you offer, you must also sell the business. You must convey the message that you are a good neighbor, an asset to the community, a friendly place. If this message is not received by the community, your advertising will not promote future purchases.

The overall success of a business is not wholly dependent upon advertising. Your full responsibility remains with your overall marketing concept. Some of the factors that can and most certainly will affect your business are:

► The general economy of the nation

► The local economy

► Competitors' activity

► Labor disputes

► The product itself

► Your company's overall appearance

► Your personnel

► Your location

► Transportation

► Weather

22

You as a businessperson must prepare your business to handle these marketing variables when planning your objectives.

GENERAL ECONOMY OF THE NATION

In most cases, the national economy is a "bellwether": as the nation goes, so goes the local economy. Be aware of what is going on nationally.

THE LOCAL ECONOMY

Although the national economy will have an effect on your local area, local events will shape your business decisions. Be politically and socially aware.

COMPETITORS' ACTIVITIES

Be aware of what actions your competition is taking. Watch their activities and keep a file on their ads. You will soon learn the types of methods they use. You will, of course, learn what to expect of them. You may want to take a trip to the library and go through last year's newspaper ads to find out when your competitors hold their special promotions.

LOCAL LABOR DISPUTES

These disputes can disrupt the community's economy. The effects of labor strikes will become apparent to business even before they actually take place. Watch them carefully.

YOUR PRODUCT

Assess each product; determine its advertisability:

► *Stage in the life cycle:* If your product is in the growth cycle, it is far more advertisable than a product in a declining cycle.

► *Geography:* Items that are good for a specific region should be advertised heavily in that region (for example, beach towels near the beach).

► *Supply:* Check supply channels to make sure you have a good supply of products available, should your advertising efforts turn the product into a hot item.

► *Market:* Make sure you know who your market is for a specific product. Do this before you advertise. You can then target that market.

► *Buying motives:* Make certain you have enough information about the product so you can explain its features and price.

► *Your store's appearance:* A clean, neat, well-lit store, with logical displays grouped by relative need, will attract a larger buying public. This makes impulse buying easy.

► *Business personnel:* The attitude of business personnel is probably the most important factor in maintaining good customer flow. Keep in mind the slogan "The customer is always right." Make certain that your refund policy, your warranty policy, your hours of operation, and your check and credit policy all favor the consumer as much as possible.

► *Location:* Of course, trying to be everywhere at one time is impossible, but maintaining a location that is convenient and highly visible is an extra assurance that your advertising dollars will be more productive.

SPECIFIC GOALS

By simply stating the previous goals, we have established objectives for your business.

It is important that you devise a *specific* goal system. Figure 3.1 displays the importance of timing to a good advertising program. A simple formula should help you determine your advertising effectiveness.

Our business will produce _____ sales at a
cost of $_____ per sale from the _____
market for _____ (product) by _____ (date).

This simple formula is as complex as it needs to get. Keep it simple.

DETERMINING THE MARKET

In the case of most retail businesses, the market for the product is already established. For example, if you sell cosmetics, you know that

make this timing test...

FIGURE 3.1

Today, merchants are keenly aware the *timing* is essential to sound, profitable advertising. Making the simple check suggested here, they are often surprised and shocked at how far out of line their advertising is.

If you want well-timed advertising to sell more merchandise at lower unit cost, you want a sales and advertising pattern which month by month looks—

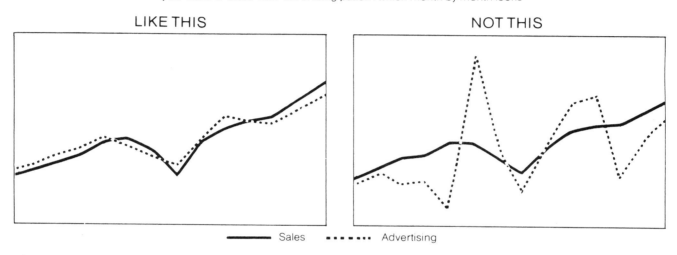

And if you want each department to deliver its maximum traffic and volume at lowest unit cost, you want a comparison that looks—

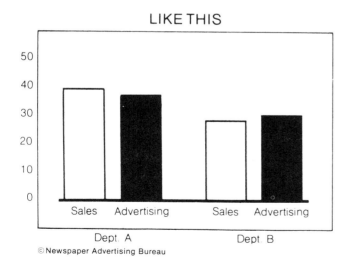
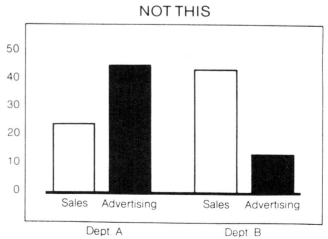

most of your customers will be women—an obvious assumption. However, markets are not always that clear-cut. Hair spray, for example, was once used only by women; now both men and women use the product. Bicycles were once only for children, now they are very popular with adults.

Home buyers were once primarily middle-aged adults with children. Now many unmarried young people are purchasing their own homes. The American consumer presents an ever-changing market.

In short, it is to the advantage of local businesses to select and identify their market precisely. A retail store should decide on a specified market and direct its advertising to that market. Select customer criteria that you know will benefit your overall sales effort. This simple form should help you target your customers.

DESIRED CUSTOMER PROFILE

AGE: 35-49   SEX: Female

AREA: 2-mile radius   SPECIAL
                                           INTERESTS: Crafts

INCOME
LEVEL: $10,000-$15,000   PROFESSION: Housewife

SPECIAL QUALIFICATIONS:

Once these criteria are established, you can use this information to match it to the media you select. You will then be able to appeal to specific customer types.

It is advisable to make a list of those customers actually received. Then you can compare the customers desired with those received.

Once you begin to advertise, you can compare the two surveys, and you can see whether your selected media is on target. Naturally, the criteria you set will depend on your business operation. Most businesses fall under one of the classifications discussed below.

> ► *Department store:* The criteria for this type
>   of store can vary from department to depart-

```
┌────────────────────────────────────────────────────────────┐
│              ACTUAL CUSTOMER PROFILE                         │
│                                                              │
│   MONTH OF    Nov.        NO. OF CUSTOMERS                    │
│                           SAMPLED:      50                    │
│                                                              │
│   AVERAGE AGE:  28-40     SEX:   21%      79%                 │
│                                  MALE    FEMALE               │
│                                                              │
│   AREA:  Approx. 5 miles  INCOME                             │
│                           LEVEL:  Average $12,000            │
│   PROFESSION:   56%                                          │
│                 Housewives                                   │
│                                                              │
└────────────────────────────────────────────────────────────┘
```

ment. Thus, your advertising must feature items from each department aimed at a particular audience. The fact that most department stores have so many varied products has always made the identification of advertising criteria a difficult and complex problem. Thus, to reach the greatest number of prospective customers, department stores have had to use many media simultaneously.

► *Specialty store:* The selection of customer criteria for this type of store is much less complex due to the small number of items and the fact that most items sold in specialty stores are related. That means that selecting the customer criteria and selecting the media to reach those potential customers are much easier.

► *Discount store:* This type of store deals primarily in price reductions. Most discount stores buy merchandise in volume quantity, thus allowing them to offer a wide range of products. Most discount-advertising appeals are aimed at the bargain hunter or lower-income shopper.

▶ *Chain store:* Like discount stores, chain stores usually have the advantage of buying at reduced prices. Their advertising reflects the lower prices, thus promoting an overall store image.

▶ *Family-owned store:* Generally, as the name implies, the business is owned by the members of one family. These stores can be combination of products and services, which may complicate the selection of customer criteria.

▶ *The mom & pop business:* These businesses can range greatly in size. Some carry a limited product line, others are an entire department store. The selection of customers' criteria must be left to the product line.

Again, each type of store must have its own customer-selection criteria. While many businesses that do not offer products for sale may be classified as retail service businesses, it is also true that there are many small to medium distribution and manufacturing businesses that use the same advertising approaches. Let's take a look at what some of these businesses are.

▶ *Distributors.* A distribution business is just as the name implies, a business of taking products that others have manufactured and finding channels of distribution for them to be sold. These types of businesses are also known as wholesalers.

▶ *Jobbers.* Many people have called jobbers and distributors the same thing. A jobber is an individual or a company of individuals that takes the product of another and actually places it in outlets so that the eventual consumer will have access to it. A distributor may use jobbers to place his or her products.

▶ *Representative firms.* These are sales firms that will take a manufacturer's product and sell it into specific companies or territories.

Many times, reps will deal directly with the end user.

► *Manufacturing.* These are firms or individuals that actually turn raw materials into finished products for consumer use. They may or may not have their own sales-force or distribution system.

As we can see, all types of business, both retail and nonretail, have very similar needs to be recognized and used. Their marketing strategies may be quite similar.

29

4
STRUCTURING YOUR ADVERTISING

It is important to understand what services advertising performs in the retail store or business. Purchasers of advertising frequently expect that advertising that runs on one day will bring the desired results on the following day. Actually, it is far more important for advertising to bring in business tomorrow, next week, next month, and next year.

The great majority of retail businesses are run by one or two people. Although such organizations would never have *full* advertising departments of their own, anyone who is responsible for developing an advertising program should understand the structure of an advertising department.

Consider all the functions that an advertising department must perform:

▸ Communicating the store personality.

▸ Indicating the store's place in the community.

▸ Building the store's name.

▸ Providing important reasons for shopping at this store as opposed to elsewhere.

▸ Explaining the merchandise.

▸ Announcing sales and special events.

▸ Building and maintaining traffic.

▸ Reaching new customers.

▸ Maintaining the flow of established customers.

All of these functions are direct responsibilities of the advertising department—even when that "department" consists of only one person. A word of caution is in order however. Advertising alone does not perform miracles—salespeople must sell, employees must be courteous, merchandise must be priced and displayed well, and company policy must favor the consumer. Advertising only communicates these factors.

Let's take a look at the way an advertising department should be structured. Figure 4.1 illustrates how a typical advertising department works.

FIGURE 4.1

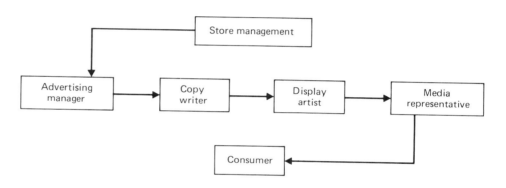

The store manager tells the advertising manager which products and services are to be advertised, the ad manager devises a campaign theme, the copy writer puts together the proper wording, and the art department puts the theme and copy into the appropriate form. The media representative then delivers the completed campaign to the medium (or media) selected by the ad manager. In a small operation all of these functions may be handled by just one person. In such cases, it is always advisable that he or she try and obtain a second opinion. It is very easy for the individual owner to become overly involved with the inside operation of the business and unable to project a true picture of that business to the public.

In order to control the advertising process it would be to the advertiser's advantage to use a development chart similar to that illustrated in Table 4.1. This will allow you to follow your advertising plan through its development.

TABLE 4.1
Advertising Development Chart

TASK	PERSON RESPONSIBLE	DATE DUE	DATE COMPLETED	PASSED TO	OK'D	REMARKS
Establish Advertising Objective						
Determine Media						
Calculate Cost						
Prepare Preliminary Copy						
Submit Rough Draft						
Review and Correct						
Submit Final Draft						
Review and Discuss						
Place with Media						
OK Proofs						
Follow Up on Ad						

SOURCES OF ASSISTANCE

While all of these functions may seem simple in theory, they can be time-consuming and, for those who are not especially creative in nature, they can also be burdensome.

At this point, we would like to make a suggestion that may be of tremendous help to you in devising your advertising plan. While it is, of course, understood that budget factors are critical in most small to medium-sized businesses, it is advisable to seek professional help with those problems that are not within the advertiser's reach. These services can be obtained on a piece-by-piece basis and usually at moderate cost.

Consider, for example, art services. This is one area that poses a problem for most businesspeople. Most businesspeople are not usually very artistic. They do not think in terms of what is effective in print. Rather, they think in terms of what appeals to them as individuals. All too often they find that what they thought was very creative did not do well in the marketplace. You can find professional help in the Yellow Pages under Art, Artists, Graphic Arts, and Graphic Design.

The average cost for a newspaper layout generally runs between $20 and $50. When weighed against the potential loss of effectiveness, art services can be a very wise investment. The same is true for radio and TV copy. Look in the Yellow Pages under Radio Production and Radio and Television Advertising Production.

One of the most common objections to using outside sources is that most newspapers and magazines and radio and TV stations will provide these services at little or no cost. The problem here is that their scope is limited. They may have hundreds of businesses advertising at the same time; they may be pressed for time; and, in some cases, their advertising art services are not up to par. Radio and TV stations have only so much talent from which to draw. Therefore, either you don't always get something you're satisfied with, or you begin to look and sound like every other advertiser.

Figures 4.2 and 4.3 illustrate some ways of compiling sales data.

ADVERTISING AGENCIES—THEIR FUNCTIONS AND USES

The decision to hire an advertising agency to handle your company's advertising must be examined closely.

First of all, the motive behind hiring an advertising agency must be regarded as suspect. In many instances, particularly in smaller businesses, the agency concept is viewed as a prestige appointment. Many businesspeople like the prestige of having an advertising agency to rely upon; it makes them appear successful in the eyes of their peers.

compare your
sales and advertising (month by month)

FIGURE 4.2

1. Write in monthly sales in the first column below. Then total.

2. Find what percentage each month contributes to annual sales by dividing annual sales total into each month's sales. Write in percentage figures. Round off to total 100% for the year.

3. Do the same for your advertising. Write in advertising used each month (either in dollars, column inches or lines). Then total.

4. Divide this total into each month's figure to get monthly percent. Again round off to total 100% for the year.

5. Plot the monthly percentages of sales and advertising on the graph below. Compare your sales and advertising. Wherever sales and advertising lines don't run close, you're missing selling opportunities with advertising that's too early or too late.

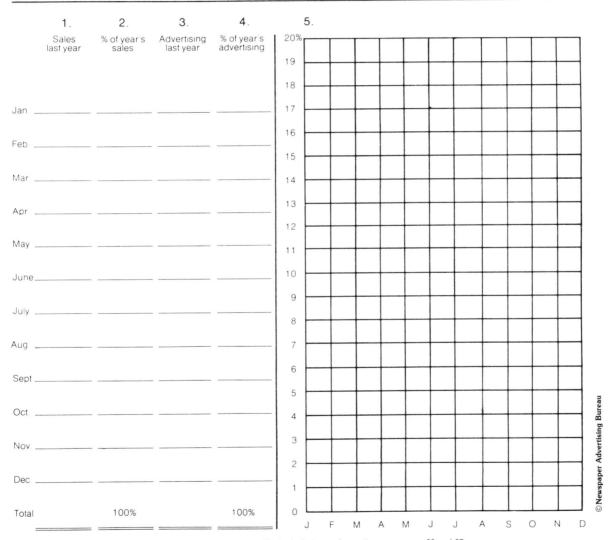

Note: If your store figures are not readily available you can use the typical store sales patterns on pages 36 and 37.

34

Yet, if the peer group has a good grasp of their own business, they will see through it if it is only an image ploy.

Secondly, many small businesses will rely on agencies just to "get rid of the problem." In effect, they have handed over their business future to someone else. Many businesspeople do not even take an active role in the advertising process once it has been turned over to an agency.

This is not meant to say that agencies are not good, or that they do not contribute to the success of a business. Many of them are excellent; and in many cases they are appropriate and helpful.

The purpose of this section is to help you determine:

► What steps to take to determine if an advertising agency is appropriate.

► How to go about selecting one.

► How to use one to the best interest and advantage of your company.

Let's examine why a business might want to use an agency. Most businesses that use agencies prefer them because:

► Agencies are specifically staffed to perform a variety of communication functions.

► Agencies can draw on a wide base of experience in a particular field or a variety of fields.

► Being from the outside, agencies frequently are able to bring in more objective views.

► Agencies generally have a better knowledge of media and how they work.

WHAT DOES AN AGENCY DO?

In most cases, particularly in the industrial field but elsewhere as well, agencies offer a wide variety of services. They generally include the following:

► Analysis of market conditions and review of company sales objectives.

total retail sales by types of stores
percent of the year's total sales done each month.

ALL RETAIL STORES
($651,884,000,000)

7 2 6 9 7 9 8 4 8 4 8 5 8 6 8 3 8 2 8 6 8 6 10 4

DEPARTMENT STORES
($68,011,000,000)

5 8 5 6 7 0 7 9 7 6 7 9 7 7 8 0 8 0 8 6 10 0 15 9

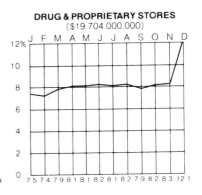

DRUG & PROPRIETARY STORES
($19,704,000,000)

7 5 7 4 7 9 8 1 8 1 8 2 8 1 8 2 7 9 8 2 8 3 12 1

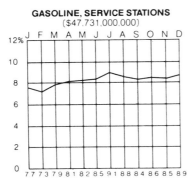

GASOLINE, SERVICE STATIONS
($47,731,000,000)

7 7 7 3 7 9 8 1 8 2 8 5 9 1 8 8 8 4 8 6 8 5 8 9

GROCERY STORES
($131,133,000,000)

8 4 7 5 7 9 8 2 8 3 8 2 8 9 8 2 8 3 8 6 8 2 9 3

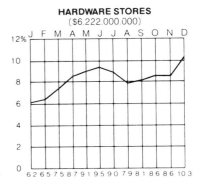

HARDWARE STORES
($6,222,000,000)

6 2 6 5 7 5 8 7 9 1 9 5 9 0 7 9 8 1 8 6 8 6 10 3

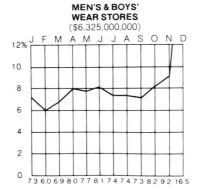

**MEN'S & BOYS'
WEAR STORES**
($6,325,000,000)

7 3 6 0 6 9 8 0 7 7 8 1 7 4 7 4 7 3 8 2 9 2 16 5

**PASSENGER CAR,
OTHER AUTOMOTIVE DEALERS**
($115,631,000,000)

6 6 7 2 8 8 9 1 8 9 9 5 9 1 8 4 7 9 8 4 8 1 8 0

SHOE STORES
($4,373,000,000)

6 9 6 2 7 5 9 4 7 7 7 7 6 8 7 9 0 8 8 8 5 12 0

FIGURE 4.3

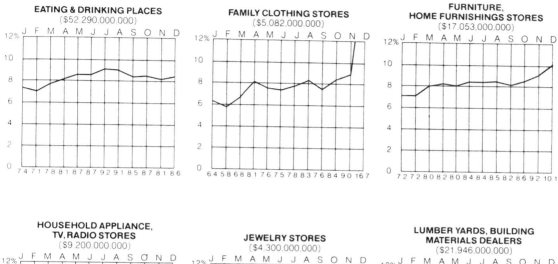

EATING & DRINKING PLACES
($52.290.000.000)

FAMILY CLOTHING STORES
($5.082.000.000)

FURNITURE,
HOME FURNISHINGS STORES
($17.053.000.000)

HOUSEHOLD APPLIANCE,
TV, RADIO STORES
($9.200.000.000)

JEWELRY STORES
($4.300.000.000)

LUMBER YARDS, BUILDING
MATERIALS DEALERS
($21.946.000.000)

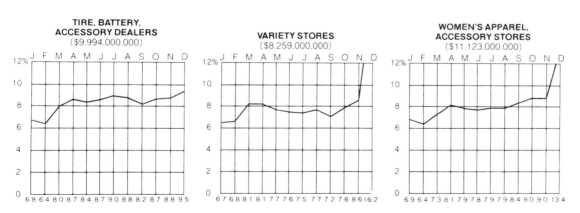

TIRE, BATTERY,
ACCESSORY DEALERS
($9.994.000.000)

VARIETY STORES
($8.259.000.000)

WOMEN'S APPAREL,
ACCESSORY STORES
($11.123.000.000)

SOURCES: U S Dept of Commerce, 1976 (Jewelry Stores-Jewelers Circular-Keystone)

37

► Recommendations concerning advertising budgets and programs, including types of media and schedules.

► Creation and production of advertising or sales materials.

► Purchase of advertising space in the appropriate media.

► Coordination of program execution.

► Evaluation of the results of advertising programs.

After reviewing the functions of an advertising agency one can readily see why there is an appeal to having an agency. However, just as all forms of advertising are not appropriate for every business, neither is an advertising agency appropriate for every business.

HOW DO WE DETERMINE THE NEED? It becomes apparent that in order to determine whether you need an advertising agency you first must have formulated your overall objectives. You must ask yourself:

► Do we have the capability of doing our advertising internally? At a realistic cost?

► What are our realistic growth projections over the next two years?

► How much money do we have to spend on advertising?

► Is there a real savings to be gained in both time and capital by using an agency?

HOW ARE AGENCIES COMPENSATED? This question is of prime consideration when contemplating the use of an agency. How do they get paid? Agencies, like any other form of business, have a variety of compensation arangements.

STRAIGHT RETAINER This type of arrangement generally calls for the client (your business) to pay the agency a flat fee or retainer, most often monthly, for a certain prespecified number of hours. In addition, the client is expected to pay for all media costs and art or production costs.

38

COMMISSION STRUCTURE

In this type of arrangement the agency is paid a commission by the media for placing the advertising with them. Generally, this commission runs between 15 percent and 20 percent of the total gross advertising bill. You as the client will be responsible for paying any production charges.

TIME CHARGES

An agency may charge for individual piecework done. This means that if you as the client have a special need, you then contract with an agency to do specific tasks, in specific time periods, for a set fee.

These illustrations are the most common forms of agency compensation. You will, of course, find many mixtures of these compensation forms. You must be prepared to select the form that will produce the best relationship to achieve your overall objectives.

CHOOSING AN AGENCY

Once you have decided that an advertising agency could be of benefit to your company you must select the proper agency.

This can be a simple matter. The best system is to act on referral. Ask someone you know and trust which agency he or she has used. If that is not possible, hold open agency-presentation meetings. Contact several agencies and invite them to make a presentation to your firm. This generally will require at least two meetings.

At the first meeting you will discover what types of work the agency has done in the past—and is currently doing—and you will have the opportunity to present your overall objectives to the agency for consideration. At the second meeting the agency will present a specific proposal which addresses your goals and defines how they may be of service to you in accomplishing those goals. This is also the time for the agency to present its compensation terms, as well as a list of past and present clients for your reference.

When checking agency references, it is always advisable to check with the local media to find out what type of relationship they enjoy. You will be amazed what you find out about agencies this way.

With the information you obtain you can then intelligently determine which agency can best serve your needs.

On the following page you will find an agency-evaluation article to assist you with selecting the proper agency.

A NEW, SIMPLER, LOWER-RISK PROCEDURE FOR SELECTING A NEW ADVERTISING AGENCY

By Robert H. Bloom,
Chairman
The Bloom
Companies, Inc.,
Dallas, Texas
(Used with permission)

Let's start with the best advice of all . . . *don't change!*

An agency change is time-consuming, expensive, and risky. A comparable investment of time, effort, and money in improving your existing agency relationship will frequently provide greater return on investment to the advertiser.

But if all efforts to improve your current agency relationship fail and a change is essential, this article sets forth a new, simpler, lower-risk selection procedure. It's new, I suggest, because this procedure does not exist in ANA or AAAA literature on the subject. It's simpler because most procedures are extremely complex. It's lower risk because the advertiser obtains the relevant information he needs to discriminate among the finalists. And it paves the way for a more effective relationship by assuring that the new agency has a clear going-in understanding of the advertiser's expectations and priorities.

In any selection procedure it is vital to avoid an unrealistic, artificial, and emotional climate at the agency presentation. It's dangerous to select an agency based on a temporary "high" stimulated by a colorful audiovisual show or a stirring exhortation by an agency principal. A two-hour agency presentation, no matter how exciting and innovative, gives no assurance of a sound, enduring, mutually productive client/agency relationship.

Therefore, any effective procedure for selecting a new advertising agency must "build in" *objective* techniques to avoid this kind of artificial environment. The following seven-step procedure does just that:

STEP 1: DEFINE YOUR NEEDS

- ► Identify each brand's high-priority needs. Make a list, in order of priority, of the top ten (maximum) specific short-term needs your new agency must satisfy. Now do the same for your long-term needs.

- ► Analyze why your current agency didn't meet your needs. Take time for introspection. List the five *real* reasons the agency is being terminated. Describe what *you* tried to do to correct each.

- ► Analyze your "avoidance requirements." Make a list, in order of priority, of the five specific

40

"factors" which must be avoided in your new agency relationship. Taboos, prejudices, personalities . . . let them all out here.

► Get agreement from *all* your decision makers on the above. The *real* decision makers.

STEP 2: IDENTIFY AGENCIES WHICH MIGHT MEET ALL YOUR NEEDS

► Start with a full list of agencies which appear to be qualified. Match your "needs" from STEP 1 against secondary data about each agency. Advertising industry trade sources are usually adequate.

► Narrow the list to only those agencies which, from the secondary data, can fully meet your needs. If you have more than ten on this list, narrow again. More than ten is unmanageable.

STEP 3: CONTACT THE BEST-QUALIFIED CANDIDATES

► Send a brief letter of introduction to the best-qualified candidates (maximum ten).

► Along with your letter provide the following:

A one-page description of your company/ brands.

A one-page summary of your short-term and long-term "needs," as defined in STEP 1.

Other relevant materials (annual report, product literature, one or two examples of current advertising, etc.).

A request to each agency for a few samples of their three (maximum) most "effective" campaigns. In one page (or less) they should tell you why each campaign was "effective."

An invitation to each agency to submit *in person* (at a meeting described below) the answers to the following two key questions: (1) Why is our account particularly attractive to your agency? (2) What are the five qualifications which make your agency the most capable resource for our account?

STEP 4: MEET WITH BEST-QUALIFIED CANDIDATES/ SCREEN TO FIVE FINALISTS

► Arrange a meeting between each agency and the persons at the client who will be the principal interface with the agency. Hold it at the agency. Tour agency facilities. Meet the agency people informally. Absolutely no presentation of any kind should be permitted, and the meeting should be limited to three hours. No reels. No "show and tell" of any kind. Just a relaxed meeting to establish dialogue between client representatives and selected members of the agency. Talk about the agency. Talk about the client. Examine the all-important "chemistry."

► Most important, review the agency's response to the two key questions in STEP 3. This will give you valuable insight into the agency's thinking process.

► Ask for three client references. Call each and probe about agency performance in areas related to your high-priority needs.

Now you should be able to narrow the list to five finalists. Any more than five will be unmanageable.

STEP 5: ARRANGE A COMPREHENSIVE BRIEFING OF ALL FINALISTS

► Invite each finalist (maximum five) to your headquarters for a comprehensive individual briefing.

► Provide each agency with the following:

More data about your firm and products, sales information, relevant research, additional examples of past advertising, etc.

Access to data about your product capabilities (plus a tour of your plant if it's accessible).

► Arrange interviews with key influentials of your organization; provide ample time for questions and answers. Encourage mutual candor.

► Provide each agency with written "specifications" (outlined below) for the final presentation. Obviously, each agency must be given the same data and access to the same people. No special considerations.

STEP 6: THE FINAL PRESENTATION

► With additional data and time to rethink your previous response to the two key questions, in what way (if at all) would you change your answers?

► Which of your existing staff members will compose the team assigned to our account? What other clients will they serve? What percentages of their time do you estimate will be allocated to our account? What previous related experience can they bring to bear on our business?

► Describe, on a single page, what you consider to be the three key marketing problems and three key marketing opportunities for our account in the next year. Do the same for long-term.

► Present a maximum of three agency case histories which clearly demonstrate an ability to deal with problems and opportunities similar to those you outlined above. This is the place to show us your proven strategic thinking and creativity. Describe the results of your campaigns. Wow us!

► Identify the priority tasks which your agency will initiate during the first twelve months you

43

deal with the problems and opportunities you've defined. Demonstrate how your work will be organized to deal with these tasks in the most efficient and effective manner.

► Define the details of the specific compensation arrangement you propose, taking into account the tasks and work schedule you have established and the staff you have proposed.

► Important! No speculative creative of any kind will be permitted. We'll evaluate your creativity by your case histories. Selection criteria will be restricted to your disciplined response to the above questions so that all agencies can be judged in the identical manner.

► Insist on a disciplined response from each agency and your own organization as well. Your presentation "specifications" must be observed. Make sure to have all presentations in your headquarters, with all client decision makers present at each meeting. A maximum of two hours devoted to each presentation and all presentations to be completed in consecutive days (to assure accurate comparison).

STEP 7:
APPOINT THE
AGENCY WHICH
HAS CLEARLY
DEMONSTRATED
A SUPERIOR
ABILITY TO
SERVE YOUR
ACCOUNT

The basis of your evaluation:

► How effectively the agency participated in the briefing session and responded to the two key questions.

► Your assessment of the "chemistry."

► Your judgment of the agency's final presentation.

At the outset, I promised a better, simpler, lower-risk procedure for selecting a new advertising agency. This procedure delivers on that promise. It also eliminates the need for "consultants."

The agency that you select from this procedure will have:

- ► A comprehensive going-in understanding of your company, its needs, its perceptions, its priorities, etc.

- ► A work plan for the first twelve months of its relationship with you.

Correspondingly, you will have:

- ► An agency which, on an objective basis, is well-qualified for your assignment.

- ► An agency which fully understands your priorities and challenges.

- ► An agency which appears to offer the "chemistry" you need and want.

- ► A specific work plan for the first twelve months of your relationship.

- ► A compensation plan that clearly sets forth the terms on which you will compensate your agency.

Sure, it's costly and time-consuming to select a new agency, whether you follow this or any other objective procedure. However, the result—an enduring, mutually productive relationship—is certainly worth the effort.

But let's end where I started—*don't* change! Invest your time and money in making your *current* agency relationship work!

5
MEDIA SELECTION— AN IMPORTANT FUNCTION

The success of an advertising program is largely determined by *where* the ad is placed. Most of your advertising expenses will go toward the purchase of space or time in the media you select.

It is fair to say that most of the cost of advertising goes to the media for placement—either space, as in the case of print media, or time, as in the case of broadcast media.

Because media expenditures will in all likelihood represent the largest single expenditure in your ad budget, media selection is one of the most important decisions in the advertising planning process. The "where-to-advertise" decision is critical.

When you select your media, you will find that competition for your advertising dollar is not always balanced. For example, it will not always be a matter of deciding which newspaper to use, or which radio or television station, or which magazines. You are just as likely to have to decide whether to buy newspapers *or* radio, magazines *or* television, or how much of your advertising budget to put into business papers and how much into direct mail. All these decisions must be based on your previously defined set of overall objectives.

Before you start planning your advertising program, ask yourself these questions:

► *To whom do I want to advertise?* Who are the people who use and benefit from my product? Who are the people who may influence others to buy?

► *Where are these people?* If your business is a local one, from how large an area can you ex-

pect to attract customers? If you are a manufacturer, what industries, trades, or professions offer the best possibilities?

The media available for use by most retail businesses range from
the town's weekly newspaper to very sophisticated publications and
broadcast sources, each with its own role in influencing the consumer.

As a first step in evaluating media sources, list those facts about
each publication or source which will be used as selection criteria. These
facts should identify the audience interests, the medium's performance
with similar type businesses, its available frequency, etc. Select a mix of
criteria that fits your company's overall objectives. Never rely on just one
criterion. Here are a few examples that may help:

► What special field does the publication serve?

► Is the publication paid for or is it a "freebie"
(for example, a free pickup "shopper" paper)?

► Is the editorial content of value to the type of
person you are trying to reach?

► How often are the publications's circulation
figures or broadcast ratings updated?

► What is the ratio of advertisements to other
features? If there are too many ads, your ad
may get lost and readers or listeners may get
bored.

► What are the comparative costs of other
sources?

► What are the chances of editorial coverage for
your business? Is your business "newsworthy"?

► What extra merchandising services are provided to your business by the publication or
source?

► What results do readership studies show?
(*Note:* Readership studies and broadcast
ratings are often made available to the advertiser by the publisher or broadcaster. You
should be wary of the information that they
provide, however, and give closer considera-

tion to those studies conducted by independent organizations.)

If you prefer, you can conduct your own independent survey using a sample of the readers, listeners, or viewers from your local area, or from your current customer list. Figure 5.1 is a sample of the questionnaire approach. This can be performed by telephone or by direct contact at shopping centers or any place there is likely to be a substantial number of people.

FIGURE 5.1

(STORE OR BUSINESS LETTERHEAD) (ADDRESS)

"This is an independent marketing and advertising survey. The results of this survey will assist us in determining what course of action to pursue with regards to our future marketing and advertising efforts. We are asking your cooperation in helping us to do a lot more for our customers. If you would be kind enough to answer the following few questions, it would be greatly appreciated.

WHICH NEWSPAPER DO YOU MOST OFTEN READ? WHICH SECTION?
HOW OFTEN DO YOU READ IT?
WHAT MAGAZINES DO YOU MOST OFTEN READ?
WHAT RADIO STATION DO YOU MOST OFTEN LISTEN TO?
WHAT TIME OF THE DAY?
WHICH TELEVISION STATION DO YOU WATCH MOST OFTEN?
WHAT TIME OF THE DAY?
ANY OTHER COMMENTS YOU WISH TO MAKE:

Would you call the sort of approach shown in Fig. 5.1 good advertising? Certainly! You're out in the community telling people you care about them as customers!

Once you have made the survey, pay close attention to the incoming results: they will tell where to find your new customers. If you use forms such as those shown in Tables 5.1 and 5.2, it will help you to organize your information.

TABLE 5.1
Competitive Monitoring

CODE:
B/W - Black & White
2C - Two Colors
L/C - Color
Sp - Special Position
6 - 60 Sec.
3 - 30 Sec.

PERIOD _____ FROM _____ TO _____

MEDIA	COMPETITION				COMPETITION				COMPETITION			
	SPACE	RADIO-TV	APPROX. COST		SPACE	RADIO-TV	APPROX. COST		SPACE	RADIO-TV	APPROX. COST	

TABLE 5.2
Media Evaluation Form

MEDIA	TOTAL CIRCULATION OR AUDIENCE	COST PER AD	COST PER THOUSANDS	FREQUENCY	TYPE OF AUDIT	INQUIRY AVERAGE

PRINT MEDIA REPORTS

If you consider advertising in print publications such as newspapers or business papers, ask for circulation statements. A circulation statement shows the total number of people who receive copies of the publication and where they live. Business papers also furnish breakdowns by industry and job titles or functions. A circulation statement may be:

► audited by an outside circulation-auditing organization;

► sworn to by the publisher, but not audited; or

► neither of the above.

CIRCULATION AUDITS

These examine subscription records or evidence of how non-paid subscriptions are controlled. They also audit the amount of paper purchased, the amount used for each issue, printing bills, and postage costs.

Remember that audits measure distribution only; they do not measure readership. Readership can be learned only by independent survey, either by the publisher, an independent research firm, or businesses (such as described earlier in this section).

Most audits are made once a year, but publishers issue circulation reports every six months. Both of the reports are audited at the same time once a year, at the time of the annual audit. If either of them is found wrong in any respect, the publisher is required to report publicly what is wrong and the correction.

Four organizations in the United States audit circulations:

The Audit Bureau of Circulations (ABC) audits daily, Sunday, and weekly newspapers; consumer magazines; farm publications; and business papers. It requires that at least 70 percent of the circulation be paid and, except for business papers, reports and audits only paid circulation.

The Business Publications Audit of Circulation (BPA) audits business papers. It audits both paid and nonpaid circulation and reports separately for each.

Certified Audits of Circulations (CAC) audits "shoppers."

Verified Audit Circulation Corp. (VAC) audits all types of publications, but mostly nonpaid types of business papers and shoppers.

You will find that not all publications are audited. The primary reason for not being audited is the cost to the publisher.

MEASURING BROADCAST AUDIENCES

Stations and program audiences for radio and television are measured by privately owned research firms using different methods of collecting data. Whereas the entire circulation of printed media is covered by audits, radio and TV audience measurements are based on samples of households or individuals in the population.

These samples are selected and the entire process is carried out using recognized statistical methods. The Broadcast Rating Council audits the reports of the major broadcast measuring services to be sure that audience measurements meet certain standards and adhere to their reported procedures.

It is quite possible that you have never been asked about your radio or television listening and do not know anyone who has been questioned. What makes a sample acceptable is whether everybody who might have been approached had an equal chance of being included in the sample.

Just what the survey findings can tell you about the audience of a broadcasting medium varies depending on how the rating service collects its data. All of them estimate the following from a sample:

▸ The number of receiving sets available and in use in specific areas at a specific time period.

▸ The share of the audience tuned into a certain station at that particular time period.

MAKING THE MEDIA DECISION

When you first look at the circulation reports and broadcast ratings, you will feel hopelessly confused. Don't become discouraged! Your media rep will help you solve the mysteries quickly. The most important thing is that you as a businessperson know that that information exists and is available to you. When you sit down to make a decision about which media to use, your first inclination will be to use all of them or at least a good many of them. Let me caution you about spreading your ad budget too thin: you may jeopardize necessary impact.

When you do select the right media, make sure that they are media that will allow you to advertise frequently and regularly. Advertising is most effective when it follows a pattern of constantly spaced repetition. Over the long run, the business that paces itself steadily will reap the biggest harvest from its advertising dollar.

NEWSPAPERS

Most advertising in daily newspapers is local advertising. In weekly newspapers and shoppers, the advertising is almost entirely local. These weeklies, together with dailies in small- and medium-sized cities and suburbs, are especially good media for retail and service advertising.

Why are newspapers good for local advertising? Basically because people like local news. The growth of suburban dailies and weeklies is not due entirely to the migration of families from the cities. Reading habits are changing. Many people now depend on radio and television for regional and national news, as well as for getting event headlines first. The local newspapers give people the details that the electronic media do not deliver. Some people still read the big-city dailies, but they also want news closer to home and of a more personal nature. For this they turn to more local publications. Many larger city newspapers are trying to respond to this need by providing their suburban readers with zone or suburban editions.

Newspapers generally have something for everyone of all ages and backgrounds. Thus, regardless of what you are selling, advertising in the newspaper will reach people who live near you and are logical customers.

Newspapers are flexible. For example, you can let the paper insert your ad wherever there is space, or you can pick sections of the paper you feel will reach your customers best. Newspapers can be flexible in the size of your ad, as well. You can offer more illustrations, and more content.

The only real question yet to be decided is which paper do you use. Let's look at some of the characteristics of newspapers. Evening papers outnumber morning papers five to one. They are generally home-delivered or picked up on the way home. They are read in greater detail than morning papers because people have more time in the evening.

Sunday newspapers are in a different category because they are made up of two segments. They offer daily news, but they also offer material that is for weekly use, such as the TV broadcast programming guide.

Newspapers can provide more detail for a longer period of time than can any other advertising media, with the exception of magazines. When shopping in the newspaper, most people will comparison shop. They will constantly compare one store, one brand, one item, one price, against the others.

Even in today's fast-paced, mobile society, the newspaper plays a major role in communicating today's retail message. Understanding the newspaper and how it is used will save many hours of valuable time.

Even though you may be familiar with your local newspaper, a quick review may help to develop some fresh new approaches.

NEWSPAPER DISPLAY AND CLASSIFIED ADVERTISING

Classified advertising appears in columns set aside for specific subjects. As you may know, the classifieds attract dedicated readers.

Display advertising is all other advertising not listed in the classified section. Display advertising is the largest category of newspapers' bulk advertising.

GENERAL AND LOCAL ADVERTISING

General advertising is not normally of a local nature. Usually a paper will charge a higher rate to those advertisers outside their area.

Local advertising is space actually paid for by local residents and establishments which sell at retail. This rate is generally much lower than the general rate.

BUYING NEWSPAPER SPACE

Securing the right to advertise in a paper is called buying space. While your newspaper representative will help you to accomplish your purchase, it is a good idea to know how to figure newspaper space.

Most newspapers sell space by what they call "agate line." There are 14 agate lines to a "column inch" *regardless* of how wide the columns are. The height of your ad (known as "depth" to the paper) is measured in ruler inches.

An ad 8 inches in depth by one column wide would measure 8 column inches. If the same ad was two columns wide, it would be 16 column inches. To connect any of these ad sizes to agate lines, simply multiply by 14. Thus, 16 column inches equals **224** agate lines.

ORDERING NEWSPAPER

When ordering newspaper space, it is advisable to place your order in writing so as not to create a misunderstanding as to size, dates, or amounts. Figure 5.2 is a sample of a Newspaper Insertion Order Form. This simple form can not only help you order your newspaper space, it will also give you an accurate record of all newspaper expenditures. Figure 5.3 shows the same form with information filled in.

NEWSPAPER RATES

Newspaper rates are determined by the publisher of each newspaper. There are no set rates among papers. In most cases, a paper will

FIGURE 5.2

TO:

HEADLINE:

ADVERTISER:

POSITION:

Please insert advertising as follows:

COPY:			INSERTION DATES			
			DAY	DATE	SIZE	RATE
	Attached	☐				
	To Come	☐				
	You Have	☐				
	Camera Ready Art	☐				
	Mat	☐				
	Cut	☐				
	Hold Material	☐				
	Return Material	☐				

SPECIAL INSTRUCTIONS:

PROOFS:

Submit_____To Advertiser

Submit_____To

TEARSHEETS:

Submit_____To Advertiser

Submit_____To

NOTE: The Advertiser on this Contract is solely liable for the total amount of the advertising run against this Contract, until payment has been made to the Agency named on this Contract. Upon receipt of all monies towards this Contract the Agency shall become solely liable for all money due the media as per this Contract, less Agency commissions.

BILLING INSTRUCTIONS:

COST:

Total Inches DAILY..... @ _____

$ _____

Total Inches SUNDAY.... @ _____

$ _____

TOTAL GROSS SPACE COST... $ _____
LESS AGENCY
COMMISSION: $ _____

TOTAL NET PAY $ _____

SUBMIT ALL INVOICES IN DUPLICATE

AUTHORIZED BY _____

MEDIA SELECTION — AN IMPORTANT FUNCTION

FIGURE 5.3

TO: ANYTOWN WATCHDOG
2848 Printit St.
Anytown, St. 55555

HEADLINE: ABC GENERAL SELLS BEST

ADVERTISER: ABC General Store
1151 Maple St.
Anytown St. 11111

POSITION: RT. Hand column sports page

Please insert advertising as follows:

COPY:			INSERTION DATES			
			DAY	DATE	SIZE	RATE
	Attached	X	Fri	12/10/79	3col X 10	3.65
	To Come	☐				
	You Have	☐				
	Camera Ready Art	☐				
	Mat	☐	Sat	12/11/79	3col X 10	3.65
	Cut	☐				
	Hold Material	☐				
	Return Material	☐				
SPECIAL INSTRUCTIONS:			Sun	12/12/79	3col X 10	4.50

PROOFS:
Submit _Before Print_ To Advertiser

Submit_____ To

TEARSHEETS:
Submit _Before Print_ To Advertiser

Submit_____ To

NOTE: The Advertiser on this Contract is solely liable for the total amount of the advertising run against this Contract, until payment has been made to the Agency named on this Contract. Upon receipt of all monies towards this Contract the Agency shall become solely liable for all money due the media as per this Contract, less Agency commissions.

BILLING INSTRUCTIONS:

Bill in triplicate will pay

net thirty days.

COST:
Total Inches DAILY..... ● _60_
$ 219.00

Total Inches SUNDAY.... ● _30_
$ 135.00

TOTAL GROSS SPACE COST... $ 354.00
LESS AGENCY COMMISSION: $ None

TOTAL NET PAY $ 354.00

SUBMIT ALL INVOICES IN DUPLICATE

AUTHORIZED BY _____

establish a sliding scale of rates. Most modern newspapers use a "lines-used" format, or a "frequency-of-insertion" rate.

LINES-USED FORMAT

Open rate	Per line:	$ 2.00
500 lines per year		1.95
1,000 lines per year		1.80
2,500 lines per year		1.70
5,000 lines per year		1.55
10,000 lines per year		1.40

Thus, if you signed a contract for a 2,500 line rate, you would pay $1.70 per line or $23.80 per column inch ($1.70 × 14 = $23.80).

Using the frequency-of-insertion formula, you would be required to run advertising space a given number of times per year.

INSERTION DISCOUNTS

Open rate	Per line:	$ 2.00
13 times a year		1.95
26 times a year		1.80
52 times a year		1.70

How do you figure the total cost of the space you're going to run? Let's say you've signed a contract for a 2,500 line rate. Using our rate card, we see that our line rate is $1.70 per line. For an ad that measures 2 columns by 7 inches, we compute as follows.

2 columns × 7 inches = 14 column inches

14 column inches × 14 (agate lines) = 616 lines

616 lines × $1.70 = $1,047.20 (total cost)

SHORT RATE

A newspaper contract is like any other contract: once you have signed it you are expected to live up to the agreement. If for some reason you cannot, or will not, most papers will charge you a short rate. What this means is that you will be billed at the per-line rate that you actually used. Conversely, if you use more space and paid the per-line rate you contracted for, you will in most cases receive a refund.

USING YOUR NEWSPAPER MORE EFFECTIVELY

For every great battle a general must prepare a "battle plan." During that battle, the general must maintain control. A football team must have a good game plan and follow through with it. On the following pages you will find your newspaper battle plan. Be a good general and stick to it.

ESSENTIALS OF A GOOD NEWSPAPER DISPLAY AD

(©Newspaper Advertising Bureau)

The most important single factor determining how many people will read any newspaper ad is the skill and technique used in preparing the ad. Readership studies have generally indicated that:

- Ad noting (awareness) increases with the size of the ad.
- People note more ads directed at their own sex.
- Color, particularly for illustrations, increases the number of readers.
- Tie-ins with local and/or special news events are effective in attracting readership.

The following suggestions for copy and layout are drawn from several studies. When effectively used, these techniques and rules generally increase readership.

1. Make Your Ads Easily Recognizable Studies have shown that advertisements which are distinctive in their use of art, layout techniques and typefaces usually enjoy a higher readership than run-of-the-mill advertising. Try to make your ads distinctively different in appearance from the advertising of your competitors—and then keep your ads' appearance consistent. This way, readers will recognize your ads even before they read them.

2. Use a Simple Layout Ads should not be crossword puzzles. The layout should carry the reader's eye through the message easily and in proper sequence: from headline to illustration to explanatory copy to price to your store's name. Avoid the use of too many different typefaces, overly decorative borders and reverse plates. All of these devices are distracting and will reduce the number of readers who receive your entire message.

3. Use a Dominant Element A large picture or headline will ensure quick visibility. Photographs and realistic drawings have about equal attention-getting value, but photographs of real people win more readership. So do action pictures. Photographs of local people or places also have high attention value. Use good artwork. It will pay off in extra readership.

58

4. Use a Prominent Benefit Headline The first question a reader asks of an ad is: "What's in it for me?" Select the main benefit which your merchandise offers and feature it in a compelling headline. Amplify this message in subheads. Remember that label headlines do little selling and always try to appeal to one or more of the basic desires of your readers: safety, fun, leisure, health, beauty, thrift, popularity. "How to" headlines encourage full copy readership, as do headlines which include specific information or helpful suggestions. Avoid generalized quality claims. Your headline will be easier to read if it is black-on-white and is not surprinted on part of the illustration.

5. Let Your White Space Work for You Don't overcrowd your ad. White space is an important layout element in newspaper advertising because the average page is so heavy with small type. White space focuses the reader's attention on your ad and will make your headline and illustration stand out. When a "crowded" ad is necessary, such as for a sale, departmentalize your items so that the readers can find their way through them easily.

6. Make Your Copy Complete Know all there is to know about the merchandise you sell and select the benefits most appealing to your customers. These benefits might have to do with fashion, design, performance, or the construction of your merchandise. Sizes and colors available are important, pertinent information. Your copy should be enthusiastic, sincere. A block of copy written in complete sentences is easier to read than one composed of phrases and random words. In designing the layout of a copy block, use a boldface lead-in. Small pictures in sequence will often help readership.

7. State Price or Range of Prices Dollar figures have good attention value. Don't be afraid to quote your price, even if it's high. Readers often will overestimate omitted prices. If the advertised price is high, explain why the item represents a good value—perhaps because of superior materials or workmanship, or extra luxury features. If the price is low, support it with factual statements which create belief, such as information on your close-out sale, special purchase, or clearance. Point out the actual saving to the reader and spell out your credit and layaway plans. If the item is not immediately available, state when delivery can be made.

8. Specify Branded Merchandise If the item is a known brand, say so in your advertising. Manufacturers spend large sums to sell their goods, and you can capitalize on their advertising while enhancing the reputation of your store by featuring brand items.

9. Include Related Items Make two sales instead of one by offering related items along with a featured one. For instance, when a dishwasher is advertised, also show a disposal.

10. Urge Your Readers to Buy Now Ask for the sale. You can stimulate prompt action by using such phrases as "limited supply" or "this week only." If mail-order coupons are included in your ads, provide spaces large enough for customers to fill them in easily.

11. Don't Forget Your Store Name and Address Check every ad to be certain you have included your store name, address, telephone number, and store hours. Even if yours is a long-established store, this is important. According to United States government statistics, one out of every ten families in your town probably moves each year. Don't overemphasize your signature, but make it plain. In a large ad, mention the store name several times in the copy.

12. Don't Be Too Clever Many people distrust cleverness in advertising, just as they distrust salesmen who are too glib. Headlines and copy generally are far more effective when they are straightforward than when they are tricky. Clever or tricky headlines and copy often are misunderstood.

13. Don't Use Unusual or Difficult Words Many of your customers may not understand words which are familiar to you. Words like "couturier," "gourmet," "coiffure," as well as trade and technical terms, may be confusing and misunderstood. Everybody understands simple language. Nobody resents it. Use it.

14. Don't Generalize Be specific at all times. Shoppers want all the facts before they buy. Facts sell more.

15. Don't Make Excessive Claims The surest way to lose customers is to make claims in your advertising that you can't back up in your store. Go easy with superlatives and unbelievable values. Remember: if you claim that your prices are unbelievable, your readers are likely to agree.

ESSENTIALS OF A GOOD CLASSIFIED AD

CLASSIFIED: A PLUS FOR RETAILERS

Classified advertising is a powerful additional medium which can work hand-in-hand with your display advertising. Display advertising works to create a need for a product or service. Classified advertising works to fill a need that already exists. Classified advertising reaches an exceptionally large market of qualified buyers, people who are ready to purchase and in search of a source. It is a perfect way to supplement, backup, and follow through on your current display program—and to build your business.

CLASSIFIED ADVERTISING MOVES MERCHANDISE

Classified advertising works well for employment, real estate, and automobiles. (Contact your local newspaper for aids that will help you develop successful classified ads in these categories.) It is also a first-rate medium for selling general merchandise. No other medium gives you an audience that is so ready to buy your merchandise or services.

Use classified advertising for:

- ► Moving additional merchandise inexpensively.

- ► Seasonal and overstocked goods.

- ► Special goods, trade-ins, broken assortments.

- ► Services.

- ► Clearance-sale items.

Both planned and unplanned purchases are made through classified advertisements. Eight out of ten classified shoppers definitely planned to buy the kind of item purchased. And two out of ten were "impulse buyers" who just came across the item purchased.

Classified readers are prime prospects. Classified attracts buyers with money to spend. Seven out of ten of these prime prospects shopped classified during the past seven days.

Families in the active, buying years (households with female homemakers under 40 years of age) have above-average exposure to classified advertising. More than three out of four families in this age group see the classified section over a seven-day period.

MAGAZINES While magazines were once on the decline, they enjoyed a tremendous comeback in the late 1970s. This has been primarily a consequence of "specialization." Previously, magazines were designed to reach a mass audience with a variety of subjects. Today magazines are published for special interests.

Special Groups:	Women, men, teens, business executives, etc.
Special Fields:	Music, stereos, cars, vacations, houses, etc.
Special Information:	Where to, how to, who, etc.

For nearly every category you can think of, there is probably a magazine published for readers who are interested in it. Trades, professions, vacations—all of these have their particular magazine.

For the retail advertiser, magazines can play a significant part in your advertising program. The criteria used for selecting a magazine are, of course, the same criteria used for selecting a newspaper:

► Does it reach the people I want as customers?

► How many people does it reach in that category?

► How often does the publication reach these people?

► Is it local enough to produce business?

The most obvious advantages of magazines are their selective readership and the fact that they may remain in the possession of the reader for a longer period of time. They are also likely to be reread and possibly passed on to other readers.

The obvious disadvantage of magazines is that advertising must be of a more institutional character or must concern a long-term event. You should also keep in mind that their lower frequency of publication means that your advertising must cover a much longer period of time.

6
INTRODUCTION TO PRINT COPY

Copy is the message content of your advertising. It includes the headline, the body text with its own structure, the legal signature or logo, and the store information. The copy content and its format are the most important factors in motivating the consumer to shop at your place of business. We refer to copy as the sales portion.

The visual part of the ad includes not only the very obvious illustrations, whether photographs or line drawings, but also the entire arrangement of the copy and artwork in relation to the space the ad will occupy. This visual relationship is called *layout*.

IMPORTANCE OF COPY

Most advertisements depend upon the copy to carry the message. However, copy is more than an arrangement of words that go into the advertising. The copy should explain the thinking behind the advertising. The layout of artwork must come from the content of the copy.

THE PSYCHOLOGY OF YOUR AD SELLING

Advertising is often the first step toward the sale. Sometimes an advertisement may be a complete sales appeal; that is, it may try to lead the reader through all of the psychological stages of attention, desire, conviction, and action. Most often, to accomplish all of these tasks within one ad is too much to expect. You will usually want to appeal to just one or two of these stages or simply to draw a response in some form of action.

But how do you convey your ideas? There are three general ways you can write your copy. These are called *copy approaches*.

First is the *factual approach,* which is a direct logical presentation of your ideas about the product, its benefits, and appeal. This is the approach most commonly used in retail advertising. It allows for full description, inclusion of unique details, and maximum information about construction and performance. All these factors contribute to effective retail copy.

You must always include along with your copy *who you are, what you have to offer, and where you can be reached.*

On the following pages you will find samples of good factual copy. These ads tell you WHO the advertisers are, and the copy gives a full description, including unique details about the product. Check the ads shown in Figs. 6.1-6.3 for the various elements needed for good factual copy.

FIGURE 6.1

FIGURE 6.2

FIGURE 6.3

THE PSYCHOLOGY OF
YOUR AD SELLING

An alternative to the factual approach is the *emotional approach.*
This method of writing takes the facts and presents them in emotion-
charged words, like save, sale, now, here. Underneath the vocabulary,
the advertising copy may be quite direct. This approach is widely used in
retail advertising. In most copy, these words will be used frequently. This
approach is sometimes called the "hard-sell approach." The examples
shown in Figs. 6.4-6.10 should provide you with some idea of how the
emotional approach works.

FIGURE 6.4

FIGURE 6.5

THE PSYCHOLOGY OF
YOUR AD SELLING

FIGURE 6.6

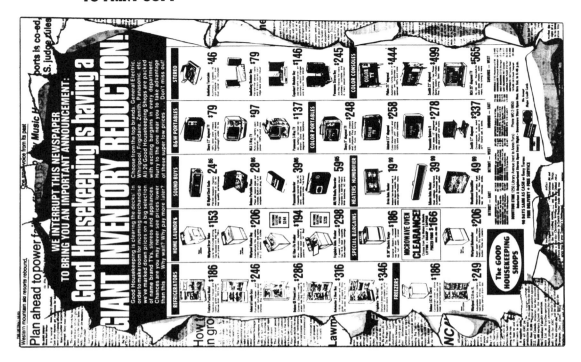

70

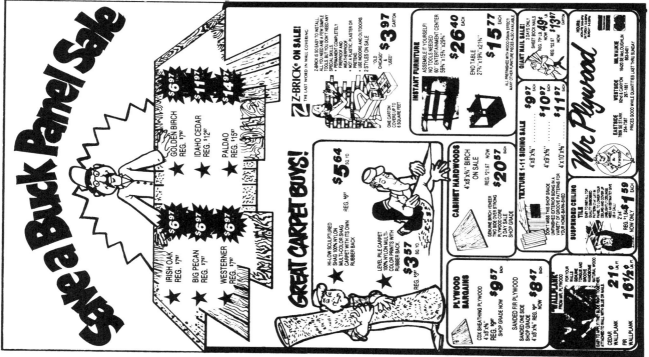

FIGURE 6.7

FIGURE 6.8

FIGURE 6.9

74

ELEMENTS OF COPY

HEADLINE   The headline is just what the name implies: the line at the head of the page. This line is generally the call to action. Many times merchants will consider good sell words to be trite so they are omitted. Here are some words that may seem old and trite, but still have great effect in a headline.

SAVE	HURRY	SERVICE	MONEY
SALE	NEED	BARGAIN	SELL
BUY	WILL		

The headline must catch the reader's attention. The reader must become interested in your ad at a glance. Watch people read a newspaper. You will soon observe that people do a lot of skimming through the paper. You must be ready to catch their attention the first time. Always make your headline brief but to the point.

BODY COPY   The body copy is used to describe the product or service in detail. This is the primary sale copy, or the heart of the advertisement. It is the body copy that carries the selling message through which the store tells its potential customers about the products or services it offers and their benefits and advantages.

Remembering the headline you have selected and the results you desire (more customer traffic, more phone calls, increased product interest), you must now create body copy that will expand upon your original headline idea. Show why your headline is believable (for example, in the case of a sale headline, you might want to put in the regular price and the sale price). You must sell the benefits of the product and the reason the customer should buy from you. Give good examples of how or where to use the items (for example, picnic baskets are great for the beach or lake). The more reasons and uses you can provide, the better your chances are of convincing a customer to buy.

EXPLAIN YOUR MERCHANDISE AND YOUR SERVICES

CLOSING   In the closing of an ad you want to exercise your command power. Ask for the sale. Use phrases such as:

HURRY IN   CALL US NOW
DON'T MISS THIS   SAVE TODAY

Don't forget to put in a good close. It will make that "extra" sale!

SIGNATURE   The signature to your ad is just like your own signature: it must remain constant and recognizable. It must also express your style of business. Therefore, you want to design a signature block that tells:

► Who you are.

► Where you are.

► How you can be reached.

► When you open and close.

Figure 6.11 shows some examples of good signatures that express the businesses in an effective light.

How can you tell if your copy is effective? By using some good advance planning you can save yourself a lot of heartache. By planning your advertising far enough in advance so that you get your finished ad back before it runs, you can pretest it.

PRETEST A pretest is performed by obtaining unbiased opinions. When you have your ad completed, test it on some of your regular customers, business associates, friends, and relatives. Show it to them. Then, without any help from you, ask them to describe what message the ad put across to them. If you receive answers that correspond with the original idea you were trying to convey, then you have an effective ad. If you don't receive the answers you were looking for, regardless of how beautiful you thought it was, go back to the drawing board before you spend money on advertising you can't use effectively. The same test applies to radio commercials too.

FIGURE 6.11

The elements of good copy include honesty, sincerity, believability, and simple but vivid vocabulary.

A good ad should be informative and explicit, interesting, enthusiastic, persuasive, memorable, and identifiable.

The combination of these elements will produce great interest in your ads.

HARD SELL vs. SOFT SELL

For years there has been great controversy within the advertising community concerning the "hard-sell" versus the "soft-sell" approach. Which is better? What is best will depend on your type of business, product, and image.

HARD-SELL APPROACH

If your type of business requires that you move items in a hurry and if the item you sell is well known to the public, you may want to use the hard-sell approach. Automobile dealers are quite proficient at using this approach. Let's examine why they are so frequently successful with this type of approach.

- ► Their product is well known. Everyone knows what a Chevrolet or a Ford is. So the emphasis is placed on sales, not on product identification.

- ► Each item must move quickly.

- ► Auto dealers hold sales frequently.

- ► Competition is high.

Figures 6.12-6.14 show excellent examples of hard-sell ads. You will notice that a lot of black ink is used. By using white space on black, you have created a reverse ad. The primary reason to use reverse is to create impact. The majority of ads run in a newspaper are printed black on white. Reverse ads enhance the attention-grabbing power of the hard-sell approach.

Notice that the large headline is selling not the product but, rather, the *theme* of the ad. The smaller copy, known as *body copy*, sells the individual product.

FIGURE 6.13

FIGURE 6.14

Counting
Down
To
Our
Grand
Opening
Soon
15 . . .
14 . . .
13 . . .

12 . . .
11 . . .
10 . . .
Counting
Down
To
Our
Grand
Opening

Counting
Down to
Opening
Our Doors
10 . . .
9 . . .
8 . . .
in the New
Century Plaza
815 Century Dr.

Telegraph Herald, Dubuque, Iowa.

All
Systems
Are
Go!

We're clearing the way to open the door for you. Watch for our **GRAND OPENING** soon.

THE CARPET SHACK

*We're Counting Down to Opening Our Doors
6 . . . 5 . . . 4 . . . in the New Century Plaza*
815 Century Drive

SOFT-SELL APPROACH

Generally speaking, the soft sell is used to inform. This approach is generally used to sell a new or unfamiliar product as opposed to a special event. For example, the clothing industry uses the soft-sell approach frequently because each piece is different.

Soft sell is also used very effectively to sell image, usually the image of quality.

FIGURE 6.15

Figure 6.15 shows examples of the soft sell.

LAYOUT Before an ad can be put together, you decide specifically what that ad is to accomplish:

► Introduce a product?

► Remind the consumer?

► Advise of a special event?

► Offer a better price?

The general message or intent will dictate the type of ad you want to produce. Once you have decided on the idea or message you wish to convey, the next step is to fashion a layout. It need not be any more in the beginning than a rough pencil sketch of your idea. Figure 6.16 is an example of a *rough*.

FIGURE 6.16

Once you have completed the rough you will need to have the layout done by an artist. Most publications will be able to have the art-work done. A completed layout will look like the example in Fig. 6.17.

FIGURE 6.17

So that the artist can put the items to be displayed in perspective, you should fill in the copy as shown on the example in Fig. 6.18.

FIGURE 6.18

TYPE SIZE When figuring your ad size, you may want to plan around the type sizes that are generally available in most publications.

Type sizes are measured in points. The smallest type is known as agate. From agate the general range runs to 72 points.

Figure 6.19 presents a handy type-size guide to help you. Figure 6.20 illustrates various type styles known as *typefaces*.

FIGURE 6.19

Helvetica Extra Compressed
Also available in 12, 14, 16, 18, 20, 40 and 48 point

22 POINT
abcdefghijklmnopqrstuvwxyz
ABCDEFGHIJKLMNOPQRSTUVWXYZ

24 POINT
abcdefghijklmnopqrstuvwxyz
ABCDEFGHIJKLMNOPQRSTUVWXYZ

28 POINT
abcdefghijklmnopqrstuvwxyz
ABCDEFGHIJKLMNOPQRSTUVWXYZ

32 POINT
abcdefghijklmnopqrstuvwxyz
ABCDEFGHIJKLMNOPQRSTUVWXYZ

6 POINT

The greatest typefaces in each of the basic letter forms, which are gothic, old-style, and modern roman, were produced before the 19th century. The first types were based on contemporary manuscript. These types were of a style we now call gothic to distinguish THEM FROM THE LATER ROMAN. THE ROMAN FORM REACHED ITS GREATEST PERFECTION IN DESIGN WITH THE TYPE OF NICOLAS JENSON IN VENICE IN 1470. SO

8 POINT

The greatest typefaces in each of the basic letter forms, which are gothic, old-style, and modern roman, were produced before the 19th century. The first types were based on contemporary MANUSCRIPT. THESE TYPES WERE OF A STYLE WE NOW CALL GOTHIC TO DISTINGUISH THEM FROM THE LATER ROMAN. THE

9 POINT

The greatest typefaces in each of the basic letter forms, which are gothic, old-style, and modern roman, were produced before the 19th century. The first types were BASED ON CONTEMPORARY MANUSCRIPT. THESE TYPES WERE OF A STYLE WE NOW CALL GOTHIC TO

10 POINT

The greatest typefaces in each of the basic letter forms, which are gothic, old-style, and modern roman, were produced before the 19th century. The FIRST TYPES WERE BASED ON CONTEMPORARY MANUSCRIPT. THESE TYPES WERE OF A STYLE WE

12 POINT

The greatest typefaces in each of the basic letter forms, which are gothic, old-style, and modern roman, were produced before the 19TH CENTURY. THE FIRST TYPES WERE BASED ON CONTEMPORARY

14 POINT

The greatest typefaces in each of the
THE GREATEST TYPEFACES IN EACH

18 POINT

The greatest typefaces in ea
THE GREATEST TYPEFACES

24 POINT

The greatest typeface
THE GREATEST TYP

30 POINT

The greatest type
THE GREATEST TY

36 POINT

The greatest ty
THE GREATES

42 POINT

The greatest t
THE GREATE

48 POINT

The greates
THE GREAT

60 POINT

The great
THE GRE

FIGURE 6.19 (Cont.)

GOTHIC BOLD
DISC 4 - NO. 2

6 POINT

The greatest typefaces in each of the basic letter forms, which are gothic, old-style, and modern roman, were produces before the 19th century. The first types were based on contemporary manuscript. These types were of a style we now call gothic to distinguish THEM FROM THE LATER ROMAN. THE ROMAN FORM REACHED ITS GREATEST PERFECTION IN DESIGN WITH THE TYPE OF NICOLAS JENSON IN VENICE IN 1470. SO

8 POINT

The greatest typefaces in each of the basic letter forms, which are gothic, old-style, and modern roman, were produced before the 19th century. The first types were based on contemporary MANUSCRIPT. THESE TYPES WERE OF A STYLE WE NOW CALL GOTHIC TO DISTINGUISH THEM FROM THE LATER ROMAN. THE

9 POINT

The greatest typefaces in each of the basic letter forms, which are gothic, old-style, and modern roman, were produced before the 19th century. The first types were BASED ON CONTEMPORARY MANUSCRIPT. THESE TYPES WERE OF A STYLE WE NOW CALL GOTHIC TO

10 POINT

The greatest typefaces in each of the basic letter forms, which are gothic, old-style, and modern roman, were produced before the 19th century. The FIRST TYPES WERE BASED ON CONTEMPORARY MANUSCRIPT. THESE TYPES WERE OF A STYLE WE

12 POINT

The greatest typefaces in each of the basic letter forms, which are gothic, old-style, and modern roman, were produced before the 19TH CENTURY. THE FIRST TYPES WERE BASED ON CONTEMPORARY MANU-

14 POINT

The greatest typefaces in each of the
THE GREATEST TYPEFACES IN EACH

18 POINT

The greatest typefaces in ea
THE GREATEST TYPEFACES

24 POINT

The greatest typeface
THE GREATEST TYF

30 POINT

The greatest type
THE GREATEST TYI

36 POINT

The greatest ty
THE GREATES

42 POINT

The greatest t
THE GREATE

48 POINT

The greates
THE GREAT

60 POINT

The great
THE GRE

6 POINT

The greatest typefaces in each of the basic letter forms, which are gothic, old-style, and modern roman, were produced before the 19th century. The first types were based on contemporary manuscript. These types were of a style we now call gothic to distinguish them from the later roman. The roman FORM REACHED ITS GREATEST PERFECTION IN DESIGN WITH THE TYPE OF NICOLAS JENSON IN VENICE IN 1470. SO PERFECT WAS THE STYLE OF HIS TYPES THAT IT BECAME THE PATTERN FOR

8 POINT

The greatest typefaces in each of the basic letter forms, which are gothic, old-style, and modern roman, were produced before the 19th century. The MANUSCRIPT. THESE TYPES WERE OF A STYLE WE NOW CALL GOTHIC TO DISTINGUISH THEM FROM THE LATER ROMAN. THE ROMAN FORM

9 POINT

The greatest typefaces in each of the basic letter forms, which are gothic, old-style, and modern roman, were produced before the 19th century. The first types were based on contemporary manuscript. THESE TYPES WERE OF A STYLE WE NOW CALL GOTHIC TO DISTINGUISH THEM FROM THE LATER ROMAN. THE ROMAN FORM

10 POINT

The greatest typefaces in each of the basic letter forms, which are gothic, old-style, and modern roman, were produced before the 19th century. The first types were based ON CONTEMPORARY MANUSCRIPT. THESE TYPES WERE OF A STYLE WE NOW CALL GOTHIC TO DISTINGUISH THEM FROM

12 POINT

The greatest typefaces in each of the basic letter forms, which are gothic, old-style, and modern roman, were produced before the 19th century. The FIRST TYPES WERE BASED ON CONTEMPORARY MANUSCRIPT. THESE TYPES WERE OF A STYLE WE

14 POINT

The greatest typefaces in each of the basic THE GREATEST TYPEFACES IN EACH OF

18 POINT

The greatest typefaces in each THE GREATEST TYPEFACES IN EA

24 POINT

The greatest typefaces in ea THE GREATEST TYPEFACE

30 POINT

The greatest typefaces THE GREATEST TYPE

36 POINT

The greatest typefac THE GREATEST TY

42 POINT

The greatest type THE GREATEST T

48 POINT

The greatest t THE GREATES

60 POINT

The greates THE GREAT

89

FIGURE 6.19 (Cont.)

GOTHIC BOLD COND.
DISC 4 - NO. 4

6 POINT

The greatest typefaces in each of the basic letter forms, which are gothic, old-style, and modern roman, were produced before the 19th century. The first types were based on contemporary manuscript. These types were of a style we now call gothic to distinguish them from the later roman. The roman FORM REACHED ITS GREATEST PERFECTION IN DESIGN WITH THE TYPE OF NICOLAS JENSON IN VENICE IN 1470. SO PERFECT WAS THE STYLE OF HIS TYPES THAT IT

8 POINT

The greatest typefaces in each of the basic letter forms, which are gothic, old-style, and modern roman, were produced before the 19th century. The first types were based on contemporary manuscript. These types were of a MANUSCRIPT. THESE TYPES WERE OF A STYLE WE NOW CALL GOTHIC TO DISTINGUISH THEM FROM THE LATER ROMAN. THE ROMAN FORM

9 POINT

The greatest typefaces in each of the basic letter forms, which are gothic, old-style, and modern roman, were produced before the 19th century. The first types were based on contemporary manuscript. THESE TYPES WERE OF A STYLE WE NOW CALL GOTHIC TO DISTINGUISH THEM FROM THE LATER ROMAN. THE ROMAN FORM

10 POINT

The greatest typefaces in each of the basic letter forms, which are gothic, old-style, and modern roman, were produced before the 19th century. The first types were based ON CONTEMPORARY MANUSCRIPT. THESE TYPES WERE OF A STYLE WE NOW CALL GOTHIC TO DISTINGUISH THEM FROM

12 POINT

The greatest typefaces in each of the basic letter forms, which are gothic, old-style, and modern roman, were produced before the 19th century. The FIRST TYPES WERE BASED ON CONTEMPORARY MANUSCRIPT. THESE TYPES WERE OF A STYLE WE

14 POINT

The greatest typefaces in each of the basic
THE GREATEST TYPEFACES IN EACH OF

18 POINT

The greatest typefaces in each (
THE GREATEST TYPEFACES IN EA

24 POINT

The greatest typefaces in ea
THE GREATEST TYPEFACES

30 POINT

The greatest typefaces
THE GREATEST TYPE

36 POINT

The greatest typefac
THE GREATEST TY

42 POINT

The greatest type
THE GREATEST T

48 POINT

The greatest t
THE GREATES

60 POINT

The greates
THE GREAT

FIGURE 6.19 (Cont.)

BALLARDVILLE BOLD
MARK UP CODE: DISC 5 NO. 1

6 POINT

The greatest typefaces in each of the basic letter forms, which are gothic, old-style, and modern roman, were produced before the 19th century. The first types were based on contemporary manuscript. These types were of a style WE NOW CALL GOTHIC TO DISTINGUISH THEM FROM THE LATER ROMAN. THE ROMAN FORM REACHED ITS GREATEST PERFECTION

8 POINT

The greatest typefaces in each of the basic letter forms, which are gothic, old-style, and modern roman, were produced before the 19th century. The first types were BASED ON CONTEMPORARY MANUSCRIPT. THESE TYPES WERE OF A STYLE WE NOW CALL GOTHIC TO

9 POINT

The greatest typefaces in each of the basic letter forms, which are gothic, old-style, and modern roman, were produced before the 19th century. THE FIRST TYPES WERE BASED ON CONTEMPORARY MANUSCRIPT. THESE TYPES

10 POINT

The greatest typefaces in each of the basic letter forms, which are gothic, old-style, and modern roman, were produced before the 19TH CENTURY. THE FIRST TYPES WERE BASED ON CONTEMPORARY MANU-SCRIPTS

12 POINT

The greatest typefaces in each of the basic letter forms, which are gothic, old-style, and modern roman, were PRODUCED BEFORE THE 19TH CENTURY. THE FIRST TYPES WERE

14 POINT

The greatest typefaces in each of
THE GREATEST TYPEFACES I

18 POINT

The greatest type faces i
THE GREATEST TYPE F

24 POINT

The greatest type fa
THE GREATEST TY

30 POINT

The greatest typ
THE GREATEST

36 POINT

The greatest t
THE GREATE

42 POINT

The greates
THE GREA

48 POINT

The greate
THE GREA

60 POINT

The grea
THE GR

FIGURE 6.19 (Cont.)

BALLARDVILLE BOLD ITALIC
MARK UP CODE: DISC 5 NO. 2

---

6 POINT

The greatest typefaces in each of the basic letter forms, which are gothic, old-style and modern roman, were produced before the 19th century. The first types were based on contemporary manuscript. These types were of a style WE NOW CALL GOTHIC TO DISTINGUISH THEM FROM THE LATER ROMAN. THE ROMAN FORM REACHED ITS GREATEST PERFECTION

8 POINT

The greatest typefaces in each of the basic letter forms, which are gothic, old-style, and modern roman, were produces before the 19th century. The first types were BASED ON CONTEMPORARY MANUSCRIPT. THESE TYPES WERE OF A STYLE WE NOW CALL GOTHIC TO

9 POINT

The greatest typefaces in each of the basic letter forms, which are gothic, old-style, and modern roman, were produced before the 19th century. The FIRST TYPES WERE BASED ON CONTEMPORARY MANUSCRIPT. THESE TYPES WERE

10 POINT

The greatest typefaces in each of the basic letter forms, which are gothic, old-style, and modern roman, were produced before the 19th CENTURY. THE FIRST TYPES WERE BASED ON CONTEMPORARY MANU-

12 POINT

The greatest typefaces in each of the basic letter forms, which are gothic, old-style, and modern roman, were PRODUCED BEFORE THE 19TH CENTURY. THE FIRST TYPES WERE

14 POINT

The greatest typefaces in each o
THE GREATEST TYPEFACES II

18 POINT

The greatest type faces i
THE GREATEST TYPE F

24 POINT

The greatest type fac
THE GREATEST TY

30 POINT

The greatest typ
THE GREATEST

36 POINT

The greatest t
THE GREATE

42 POINT

The greatest
THE GREA'

48 POINT

The greate
THE GRE/

60 POINT

The gred
THE GR.

6 POINT

The greatest typefaces in each of the basic letter forms, which are gothic, old-style, and modern roman, were produced before the 19th century. The first types were based on contemporary MANUSCRIPT. THESE TYPES WERE OF A STYLE WE NOW CALL GOTHIC TO DISTINGUISH THEM FROM THE LATER ROMAN.

8 POINT

The greatest typefaces in each of the basic letter forms, which are gothic, old-style, and modern roman, were produced before the 19th century. THE FIRST TYPES WERE BASED ON CONTEMPORARY MANUSCRIPT. THESE TYPES

9 POINT

The greatest typefaces in each of the basic letter forms, which are gothic, old-style, and modern roman, were produced before THE 19TH CENTURY. THE FIRST TYPES WERE BASED ON CONTEMPORARY

10 POINT

The greatest typefaces in each of the basic letter forms, which are gothic, old-style, and modern roman, were PRODUCED BEFORE THE 19TH CENTURY. THE FIRST TYPES WERE

12 POINT

The greatest typefaces in each of the basic letter forms, which are gothic, old-style, and modern ROMAN, WERE PRODUCED BEFORE THE 19TH CENTURY.

14 POINT

The greatest typefaces in e THE GREATEST TYPEFAC

18 POINT

The greatest type fac THE GREATEST TYP

24 POINT

The greatest type THE GREATEST

30 POINT

The greatest t THE GREATE

36 POINT

The greates THE GREAT

42 POINT

The greate THE GREA

48 POINT

The grea THE GRE

60 POINT

The gre THE GI

FIGURE 6.19 (Cont.)

UNIVERS BOLD COND. ITALIC
MARK UP CODE: DISC 5 NO. 6

6 POINT

The greatest typefaces in each of the basic letter forms, which are gothic, old-style, and modern roman, were produced before the 19th century. The first types were based on contemporary manuscript. These types were of a style we now call gothic to distinguish them from the later roman. The roman FORM REACHED ITS GREATEST PERFECTION IN DESIGN WITH THE TYPE OF NICOLAS JENSEN IN VENICE IN 1470. SO PERFECT WAS THE STYLE OF HIS TYPES THAT IT BECAME THE PATTERN FOR

8 POINT

The greatest typefaces in each of the basic letter forms, which are gothic, old-style, and modern roman, were produced before the 19th century. The first types were based on contemporary manuscript. These types were of a style we now CALL GOTHIC TO DISTINGUISH THEM FROM THE LATER ROMAN. THE ROMAN FORM REACHED ITS PERFECTION IN DESIGN WITH THE TYPE OF

9 POINT

The greatest typefaces in each of the basic letter forms, which are gothic, old-style, and modern roman, were produced before the 19th century. The first types were based on contemporary manuscript. These TYPES WERE OF A STYLE WE NOW CALL GOTHIC TO DISTINGUISH THEM FROM THE LATER ROMAN. THE ROMAN FORM REACHED

10 POINT

The greatest typefaces in each of the basic letter forms, which are gothic, old-style, and modern roman, were produced before the 19th century. The first types were based on contemporary MANUSCRIPT. THESE TYPES WERE OF A STYLE WE NOW CALL GOTHIC TO DISTINGUISH THEM FROM THE LATER

12 POINT

The greatest typefaces in each of the basic letter forms, which are gothic, old-style, and modern roman, were produced before the 19th century. The first TYPES WERE BASED ON CONTEMPORARY MANUSCRIPT. THESE TYPES WERE OF A STYLE

14 POINT

The greatest type faces in each of
THE GREATEST TYPE FACES IN

18 POINT

The greatest type faces in eac
THE GREATEST TYPE FACE:

24 POINT

The greatest type face
THE GREATEST TYPE

30 POINT

The greatest type fa
THE GREATEST TYI

36 POINT

The greatest type
THE GREATEST

42 POINT

The greatest
THE GREATES

48 POINT

The greates
THE GREAT

60 POINT

The greates
THE GREAT

94

CORNET BOLD
MARK UP CODE: DISC 5 NO. 8

FIGURE 6.19 (Cont.)

6 POINT

The greatest typefaces in each of the basic letter forms, which are gothic, old-style, and modern roman, were produced before t. century. The first used were based on contemporary manuscript. These types were of a style we now call gothic to distinguis; from the later roman. The roman form reached its greatest perfection in design with the type of Nicholas Jenson

8 POINT

The greatest typefaces in each of the basic letter forms, which are gothic, old-style, and modern roman, were produced before the 19th century. The first types were based on contemporary manuscript. These types were of a style we now call gothic to distinguish them from the later roman.

9 POINT

The greatest typefaces in each of the basic letter forms, which are gothic, old-style, and modern roman, were produced before the 19th century. The first types were based on contemporary manuscript. These types were of a style we now call gothic to distinguish them from the later roman.

10 POINT

The greatest typefaces in each of the basic letter forms, which are gothic, old-style, and modern roman, were produced before the 19th century. The first types were based on contemporary manuscript. These types were of a style we now call gothic to distinguish them from the later roman.

12 POINT

The greatest typefaces in each of the basic letter forms, which are gothic, old-style, and modern roman, were produced before the 19th century. The first types were based on contemporary manuscript. These types were of a style we now call gothic to distinguish them from the later roman.

14 POINT

The greatest typefaces in each of the basic letter

18 POINT

The greatest type faces in each of the t

24 POINT

The greatest type faces in each o

30 POINT

The greatest type faces in

36 POINT

The greatest type fac

42 POINT

The greatest type f

48 POINT

The greatest typ

60 POINT

The greatest

95

FIGURE 6.20

SERIF GOTHIC BOLD — 18 POINT
ABCDEFGHIJKLMNOPQRSTUVWXYZ
abcdefghijklmnopqrstuvwxyz
12345678910

TIFFANY LIGHT — 18 POINT
ABCDEFGHIJKLMNOPQRSTUVWXYZ
abcdefghijklmnopqrstuvwxyz
12345678910

**TIFFANY DEMI — 18 POINT
ABCDEFGHIJKLMNOPQRSTUVWXYZ
abcdefghijklmnopqrstuvwxyz
12345678910**

PACKARD — 18 POINT
ABCDEFGHIJKLMNOPQRSTUVWXYZ
abcdefghijklmnopqrstuvwxyz
12345678910

PACKARD BOLD — 18 POINT
ABCDEFGHIJKLMNOPQRSTUVWXYZ
abcdefghijklmnopqrstuvwxyz
12345678910

HOLLAND SEMINAR — 18 POINT
ABCDEFGHIJKLMNOPQRSTUVWXYZ
abcdefghijklmnopqrstuvwxyz
12345678910

FIGURE 6.20 (Cont.)

Phototypositor Type Styles

The following type styles are available in the sizes shown next to the font designation. Each style may be expanded, condensed, italicized or back slanted up to 40%. When ordering please indicate the size and special characters desired

MINIMUM CHARGE $2.50

B7 — 18 point - 144 point

DISPLAY Type faces are both varied and interestin

B11 — 18 point - 144 point

DISPLAY Type faces are both varied and

C1—18 point-144 point

DISPLAY Type faces are both varied an

TA4—18 point-144 point

DISPLAY Type faces are both varie

TA6—18 point-144 point

DISPLAY Type faces are both varie

F51—18 point-120 point

DISPLAY Type faces are both varie

FIGURE 6.20 (Cont.)

F5—18 point-120point

DISPLAY Type faces are botl

TH5—18 point-120 point

DISPLAY Type faces are b

TT10—18 point-144 point

DISPLAY Type faces are b

TV5—18 point-120 point

DISPLAY Type faces

B16—18 point-120 point

DISPLAY TYPE FACES ARE BOT

Vanguard Lite — 18 point - 144 point

DISPLAY Type faces are both varie

*The following special characters are available in both Vanguard Lite
and Vanguard Bold. Please indicate clearly which characters you wish to use.*

A A CA CA © EA FA FR GA HT KA LA LA LA LL M NT RR RA
SS ST ST TH UT V V W e ff fi fl ffi ffl I v v w y

Vanguard Demi-Bold — 18 point - 144 point

DISPLAY Type faces are both va

FIGURE 6.20 (Cont.)

H7—18 point-144 point

DISPLAY Type faces are both varied a

H9—18 point-144 point

DISPLAY Type faces are both vari

CB5—18 point-120 point

DISPLAY Type faces are bo

TB2—14 point-96 point

DISPLAY Type faces are both varie

TT4—18 point-144 point

DISPLAY Type faces are both va

Americana — 18 point - 144 point

DISPLAY Type faces ar

TB11—18 point-144 point

DISPLAY Type faces are h

H20—14 point-96 point

DISPLAY Type fa

TF17—18 point-120 point

DISPLAY Type face

FIGURE 6.20 (Cont.)

Bookman Med. — 18 point - 120 point

DISPLAY Type faces are both varie

Bookman Bold Italic W/swash — 18 point - 96 point

DISPLAY Type faces are both

The following swash characters are available with Bookman Bold Italic.
Please indicate clearly the ones you wish to use.

A A ABCG DEFGHIJKKLMM MNN NPR
R R RSS ST U VWXY Y& &*fi f fihknr r r r sw wiy

A6—18 point-144 point

Display type faces are both varied and interesting in

A10—18 point-120 point

Display type faces are both varied and interesting in co

Formal Script — 18 point - 144 point

Display type faces are both varied ana

A65—18 point-144 point

DISPLAY Type faces are both varied and interes

FIGURE 6.20 (Cont.)

A21—18 point-120 point

DISPLAY Type faces are both varied and interesting in con

A35—18 point-120 point

DISPLAY Type faces are both varied and

A49 — 18 point - 120 point

DISPLAY Type faces are both

A54—18 point-120 point

DISPLAY Type faces are bo

Keynote — 18 point - 120 point

Display type faces are both varied and in

Uranus — 18 point - 96 point

Display Type Faces Are Both Varied and

11Y2—24 point-144 point

DISPLAY Type faces are both varied and intere

F4—18 point-144 point

DISPLAY Type faces are both varied and interesting

123 —18 point-144 point

DISPLAY Type faces are both varie

Cooper — 18 point - 144 point

DISPLAY Type faces are bot

Windsor — 18 point - 144 point

DISPLAY Type faces are bot

Windsor Bold Cond. — 18 point - 144 point

DISPLAY Type faces are both varied and inter

Souvenir — 18 point - 144 point

DISPLAY Type faces are both var

Korinna — 18 point - 120 point

DISPLAY Type faces are bot

123 —18 point-120 point

DISPLAY Type faces are b

14 -14 point-108 point

DISPLAY Type faces

FIGURE 6.20 (Cont.)

FIGURE 6.20 (Cont.)

TB21—14 point-96 point

DISPLAY Type faces are both var

CK5 —14 point-96 point

DISPLAY Type faces are b

TA8 —18 point-144 point

DISPLAY Type faces are both varied and in

Shaw Text — 18 point - 86 point

DISPLAY Type faces are both varied

K19—18 point-144 point

DISPLAY Type faces are both varied and

Quilt — 18 point - 120 point

DISPLAY Type faces are both varied

M11—18 point-144 point

DISPLAY TYPE FACES ARE BOT

J5—14 point-96 point

DISPLAY Type faces are both varied and

FIGURE 6.20 (Cont.)

Tournament — 18 point - 120 point

DISPLAY Type faces are

Victoria — 18 point to 144 point

DISPLAY Type faces are both var

Robusta — 18 point to 144 point

DISPLAY Type faces are both varied

Hobo Gothic — 18 point - 144 point

DISPLAY Type faces are both varied

Ad Gothic — 18 point - 96 point

DISPLAY Type faces are both

Serif Gothic — 18 point - 144 point

DISPLAY Type faces are both vari

Celtic — 18 point - 120 point

DISPLAY Type faces are both varied

Skjold — 18 point - 96 point

DISPLAY Type faces are both

FIGURE 6.20 (Cont.)

FUTURA INLINE—18-120 point

DISPLAY TYPE FACES ARE BOT

LYDIAN BOLD—18-120 point

DISPLAY Type faces are both varie

CLOISTER BLACK—18-144 Point

DISPLAY Type faces are both va

WEEDON—18-144 Point

DISPLAY Type faces are both varied and

BRUSH—18-144 Point

DISPLAY Type faces are both va

TS8—18-120 point

DISPLAY Type faces are both varied and interesting ir

TS7—18-96 point

DISPLAY Type faces are both varied and interest

CORONET—18-144 Point

Display type faces are both varied and interesting in co

FIGURE 6.20 (Cont.)

L25—18-144 Point

DISPLAY Type faces are bo

L21—18-144 Point

DISPLAY Type faces are both

ROPE—18-120 point

DISPLAY Type faces are both varied an

KALLIGRAPHIA—18-144 Point

DISPLAY Type faces are bo

PIONEER—18-144 Point

DISPLAY TYPE FACES ARE

C5—18-96 point

DISPLAY Type faces a

OPEN COUNTRY—18-144 Point

DISPLAY TYPE FACES A

BOCKLIN—18-120 point

DISPLAY Type faces are b

FIGURE 6.20 (Cont.)

E3—18-96 point

DISPLAY TYPE FAC

TIFFANY—18-144 Point

DISPLAY Type faces a

NEW CHINA—18-120 point

DISPLAY Type faces are both varie

UNICIAL—18-144 Point

display type faces ar

E4—18-96 point

DISPLAY TYPE FAC

A12—18-120 point

Display type faces are both varied and inte

AMERICANA ITALIC—18-96 point

DISPLAY Type faces are

A23—18-120 point

Display type faces are both varied and interesting in concept and

BETTER
TYPOGRAPHY

LAYOUTS   Every piece of composition that contains more than one element should begin with a layout. The extent to which a layout should be "finished" depends upon the nature of the work. Perhaps the safest rule is, "The layout should be *adequate*." An ordinary piece of composition may require only a few lines in a rough sketch; an involved advertisement may require a close approximation of the finished ad.

When preparing the layout the goal is accuracy. When the measure is to be 23 picas, draw the sketch to that size—it is no more difficult than drawing it to 20 or 26 picas. Plates should be keyed and indicated in the proper size, shape, and position in relation to the type.

If a headline is indicated, be certain it will fit. Specifying a 48-point face which will not fit in the measure immediately pushes costs up because it means resetting in a smaller size, a different face, or a wider measure. Any one of these may yield an unsatisfactory result, with consequent further resetting of the heading.

In all cases where the fit of display lines is doubtful, the letters should be carefully drawn for size, although they need not necessarily be accurate in contour. Copy that must fit within a definite space also should be carefully calculated. The exact amount of space desired between lines, and around plates and borders may be marked on the layout.

TYPE   The height of type is 0.918 inch. Cuts, stereotypes, and elec-
MEASUREMENTS   trotypes to be printed alongside actual type must be ordered blocked on wood or metal so that they are type high.

Typographers measure type by points. One point is 0.01384 inch, and 72 points are almost exactly one inch. Actually, an area 12 × 72 points falls 4 points short of equalling 12 inches. Points are used in measuring type sizes and leads. These lines are set in 11-point type.

The pica, equal to 12 points, is used in measuring the length of type lines, the width of margins, and the depth of columns. These lines are 30.5 picas wide.

An em is another kind of measurement. It is the square of the height of the body of any type size. Thus, a 1-em quad in 9-point type is 9 points square. In 14-point type it would be 14 points square. Paragraph indentions are usually marked in ems. An en is half an em.

108

COPY FITTING

NUMBER OF CHARACTERS IN MANUSCRIPT

Typewriters are so designed that each character receives the same space horizontally, either ten or twelve characters to the inch. Multiply the number of characters to the inch by the average inches to a typewriter line. Multiply the average number of characters per line by the number of lines.

EXAMPLE: A manuscript has an average of 64 characters to the line and 25 lines to the page. Therefore, on 10 pages there are 64 × 25 = 1600 × 10 = 16,000 characters.

The short lines at the ends of paragraphs can be counted as full lines because there will be similar short lines when set in type. *Exception:* If there is a large difference between the width of manuscript and the width of type—say the manuscript averages 70 characters to the line and the type 30—this will not average out, as type set in short measures requires more letterspacing with a consequent gain in type lines.

TO FIND NUMBER OF LINES OF TYPE

Select your typeface, size, and length of line. Find its alphabet length and then refer to the Characters by Picas for the average number of characters per line. Spaces between words and punctuation points count as characters. Divide this into the number of characters in your manuscript.

EXAMPLE: We will set the manuscript of the previous example in 10-point News Gothic Condensed, 18 picas wide. Referring to the right-hand corner of each specimen page (characters to inch)— (1 inch = 6 picas)—we see that this will average 51 characters to the line. The solution is: 16,000 ÷ 50 = 320 lines.

TO FIND DEPTH IN PICAS

Multiply the number of lines by the fractional relationship which the body size of type bears to 12. For example, 6-point is one-half, 8-point is two-thirds, 10-point is five-sixths, 12-point is one, and 14-point is one and one-sixth of 12.

EXAMPLE: We are setting 320 lines of 10-point: 320 times five-sixths equals 266 picas and 8 points, which will be the depth of the column. Or, for depth in inches, an approximate depth may be had by dividing the number of lines to the inch into the number of lines. Six-point runs 12 lines to the inch, 8-point runs 9 lines, 10-point runs 7 lines, 12-point runs 6 lines, and 14-point runs approximately 5 lines. Thus 320 lines of 10-point will make approximately 320 ÷ 7, or 46 inches.

IF MATTER IS LEADED

Leading does not affect the number of lines, but it does affect the depth in picas or inches. Be careful to use body size instead of face size. Ten-point, leaded 2 points, is on a 12-point body.

EXAMPLE: If the manuscript of the previous example is to be set in 10-point 2-point leaded, it is on a 12-point body and will therefore be 320 picas deep. In inches it would make 320 ÷ 6, or 53 1/3 inches.

SPACING

Characters by Inches are all based on close spacing, which is always to be recommended, not only for economy of space but also for appearance.

LENGTH OF LINE

In body matter, the recommended length of line is about 40 characters in any size. Lines of less than 30 or more than 50 characters should be avoided as a general rule.

EXAMPLE: The ideal measure for 10-point News Gothic Condensed would be 15 picas. It should seldom be set narrower than 10 picas or wider than 18 picas.

TYPING TO FIT

If typeface, size, and measure are determined in advance, the copy can be sent to your typographer typed with the proper number of characters to the line so that the proof will run practically line for line with it.

EXAMPLE: Type is to be set in 10-point News Gothic Condensed, 18 picas wide. The typist should set the typewriter for a 51-character average length line.

MARKING
PROOFS

Symbols used to mark corrections on proofs should be clear-ly indicated with colored pencil and should be the standard proofreading marks universally used. A chart illustrating these symbols and their use is shown in Fig. 6.21.

FIGURE 6.21
Proofreaders' marks

	align type		lower
X	broken letter		lower-case letter
	close up		move to left
	close up and insert space		move to right
	delete		paragraph
	delete and close up		push down space
	hair space between letters		query to author
	indent 1 em		raise
	insert apostrophe		reverse
	insert colon		run in same paragraph
	insert comma		set in boldface type
em/	insert em dash	caps	set in capitals
en/	insert en dash	ital.	set in italic type
	insert hyphen	lc	set in lower case
?/	insert interrogation point	rom.	set in roman
ldr	insert lead between line	sc	set in small capitals
∧	insert margin addition	V∧	space evenly
	insert semicolon	sp	spell out
⊙	insert period		straighten line
	insert quotation marks	tr	transpose
#	insert space		use ligature
stet	let it stand	wf	wrong font

All marks and instructions should be made in the margin. Draw a line from the error to the symbol in the margin, being careful that lines do not cross.

If no changes are made on the proof, write "OK," initial it, and return it with any further instructions. When changes are required, mark them, write "OK as corrected" or "show revised proof" as the case may be, add your initials, and return the proof.

Corrections given over the telephone are likely to result in errors and subsequent loss of time.

STANDARD TRADE PRACTICES

Quotations are for labor only unless otherwise specifically stated, and are valid for 60 days only unless renewed in writing. Quotations are based on the prevailing scale of wages, hours of work, cost of materials, and tax rates. Quotations made verbally in person or by telephone must be later confirmed in writing to be binding. Estimates are approximations only, not to be confused with written quotations. All agreements are made and orders accepted contingent upon strikes, fires, accidents, or other causes beyond the typographer's control.

Charges are made either on an hour or piece-rate basis at the option of the typographer or as provided in quotations and will be so invoiced. Experimental work performed on order or at the request of customers, including layouts, artwork, trial composition, and proofs, will be charged. No work will be done on a speculative basis. Changes from the copy as originally submitted involve a change in quotation. Composition is set in accordance with the copy as furnished. Author's alterations in the composition or layout result in an additional charge. When style and type are left to the best judgment of the typographer, customer's changes from that style and type are author's alterations and will be so billed. Layouts and dummies submitted by the typographer remain his or her property, and no use of them shall be made or ideas taken from them by the customer, except upon payment of compensation to be determined by the typographer. This work is chargeable and will be covered by invoice.

Overtime will be charged for all work required to be done outside of the typographer's regular working hours, based on the typographer's overtime hourly selling rates.

Cancellation of regularly entered orders cannot be accepted except on terms that compensate the typographer against work done and for obligations entered into.

112

Terms are 30 days net. Accounts beyond 30 days are C.O.D. at the option of the typographer. Credit shall be extended only to firms with established rating or satisfactory reference. Running jobs (books, etc.) may be billed each month for the amount completed each month, or on which proofs are held out. C.O.D. jobs must be paid for upon delivery of first proofs.

Foundry type intended for printing, for stereotyping, for lead-mold electrotypes, or for more than four wax-mold electrotypes must either be charged for or plated and the cost of plating charged to the job.

Monotype-cast hand-set type and spacing material used in made-up jobs intended for printing will be charged.

Special material such as type, rules, special matrices, and cuts, bought at the request of the customer must be paid for by the customer at not less than 20 percent above the net cost of same.

Metal delivered to customers in the form of machine composition or made-up into pages or forms shall remain the property of the typographer until all obligations of the customer as provided for in the prevailing custom for the payment for and/or return of metal have been completely satisfied. Made-up jobs must be returned intact to receive full credit. Linotype and monotype metal, except when returned intact in made-up jobs, must be separated when returned to receive full credit. All mixed metal (loose type, leads, slugs, and rules) will, on return, be credited. Zinc or harmful chemicals will be classed as "junk" metal and will be credited as such.

Customer's property, such as copy, artwork, plates, and electros, is placed with the typographer at the customer's risk, and the typographer is not liable for loss or damage due to fire, water, theft, rodents, strikes, or other causes beyond the typographer's control. Engravings and electrotypes held beyond six months will be considered dead unless the customer instructs otherwise.

Standing type or forms kept beyond seven days for any reason, and forms or pages held at customer's request longer than 60 days, will be subject to a storage and metal rental charge. Forms returned after electrotyping and reproduction proof forms are assumed to be dead and after seven days may be distributed unless otherwise ordered in writing.

Lien is held by the typographer against all type, cuts, plates, paper, or other materials belonging to the customer as security until all just claims against the customer have been satisfied.

Proofs submitted should be read by the customer and marked "OK" or "OK with corrections." Corrections should be properly indicated and proof signed by the name or initials of the person authorized to pass on the work. If revised proof is desired, request should be made when first proof is returned to typographer. Proofs of various kinds and for reproduction are charged for at the typographer's established rates. No responsibility is assumed for telephoned correction of errors. No financial responsibility is assumed for errors, other than resetting corrections without charge.

If you are a manufacturer and advertise in business papers with distant headquarters, having a local typographer set your advertisement will give you better control over its appearance. You can know how the advertisement will look when it comes out. But wherever you have the type for your advertisements set, be sure the copy is exactly as you want it *before* you turn it over to the printer. "AA's," as printers call author alterations, will run up your costs.

When printers give you a price estimate, they assume that the copy you have submitted is the final draft. If when the proofs are submitted for your approval you make any changes other than correcting typesetting errors, the cost is added to the quoted price. The time to make changes is before the copy has been transformed into type, either metal or film. A minor change can cost more than you think.

7
RADIO AND TELEVISION

Radio and television are carrying an increasing volume of local advertising, especially retail advertising, as small-business owners recognize that more and more of their prospective customers belong to generations who expect to receive much of their information from the broadcast media. The time they spend reading may be only a fraction of the hours they spend with electronic companions—listening, watching. To reach them, small-business owner/managers may discover that it is necessary to augment—if not replace—their print advertisements with radio or television advertisements.

Radio advertising, of course, has long been a workhorse for local business. Time on national television is obviously too expensive for most small businesses. Time on local television networks, however, may be cost-effective relative to the size of the audience reached.

ADVANTAGES OF BROADCAST ADVERTISING

Radio and television allow you to aim accurately at your advertising target. They give you *flexibility* to appeal to specific types of prospects: teenagers, home workers, young adults, or whatever group you hope to attract as customers. These media can help you zero in on the customers potentially most responsive to your product, service, or store much the way special-interest magazines do.

Most radio stations' programming is designed to appeal to particular segments of the population. Similarly, individual television programs appeal to specific, presumably identifiable, groups of people. When you use radio and television, your audience is preselected; some segments of the population will be eliminated by your choice of radio station or television show. Spotting your advertising like this can be attractively cost-effective.

Radio and television are geared for *quick changes*. If you deal in seasonal products, for example, the station may be able to make automatic changes in your advertising to match changes in the weather. Is it hot? Then your air-conditioner advertisement goes on the air. Is a winter storm approaching? Then your advertisement for snow tires appears. Naturally, both broadcast media prefer to receive reasonable notice of changes, but they can provide such sudden switches.

The human voice over the air can establish a friendly rapport with listeners. It can be more persuasive than cold print. A women announcer can impart a feminine touch to commercials for products of special interest to women. Some advertisers broadcast their own commercials to give them a special impression of personal sincerity.

The human voice can also convey a sense of urgency. If you want an immediate response, your advertising message can end with a suggestion that listeners phone right away. When spoken in a conversational manner and repeated frequently, broadcast advertising is remembered.

Television advertising most closely resembles personal selling. This is because it is the only medium that combines sight, color, motion, and sound. In addition, it comes right into the home. With television advertising you can explain and at the same time demonstrate what you are selling in thousands of homes simultaneously. Since your presentation is rehearsed—or should be—you can make every second count. You can show your product in realistic settings. Your personality can be injected into your advertising.

Broadcast advertising can also help you *build your image*. Little looks as "big" as big when everyone is limited to 60 (often 30) seconds or less. When you use the broadcasting media there are no other advertisements to overshadow yours—there is nothing comparable to the full-page or double-page color advertisement to distract prospects from your fractional page in print media. When your advertisement is broadcast, the air time that you have bought is yours alone. With a little creativity, your message can be as impressive as that of the largest of your competitors.

DISADVANTAGES OF BROADCAST ADVERTISING

The most serious problem with broadcast advertising is that your potential customers have to be listening or watching during those seconds your message is being transmitted or even the most creative advertisement is useless. Another disadvantage is that the audience cannot cut out your broadcast advertisement to take along as a shopping reminder or guide. Finally, you are limited to brief copy. Your message never lasts more than a minute.

For these reasons, repetition is important in broadcast advertising. But it does, of course, cost money. What many advertisers with limited budgets often do is use broadcast ads to supplement and call attention to their advertising in print media. This often produces excellent results.

PROBLEMS IN PLANNING BROADCAST ADVERTISING

Broadcast advertising is somewhat harder to plan than advertising in printed media. In newspapers and magazines, space units are standardized. With few exceptions, the terms used and the pattern of locations in the publication on which rates are based are fairly well standardized.

In broadcast advertising, on the other hand, you will find a confusion of terms. For instance, "Class A" means prime time or "drive time" on most radio stations, but the exact hours it covers are not always the same. When you are talking with a station sales representative be certain that the terms used mean the same thing to both of you. Study rate cards carefully to learn the exact meaning of the terms.

The biggest problem in planning is obtaining the time slots and programs you want. In print media, space is expandable. Pages can be added to take care of almost any number of advertisers. But broadcasting time is limited. There are only 24 hours in a day, and some stations are licensed to be on the air only from sunrise to sunset.

Don't be surprised if other advertisers have the best time slots sewed up and intend to keep them. You may have to wait a long time to get the one you want. You might have to choose between taking a less desirable time slot and turning to other media. If you are convinced that television or radio is what you need, it is probably better to compromise on the time slot. Then, when a better time opens up, you will be in line for priority treatment.

SELECTING STATIONS

By selecting the *station,* the *program* and the *time* of the broadcast, you can reach almost any group of buyers you want. Stations attract audiences. Different programs attract different audiences. And the time of the program determines not only who is listening but also the size of the audience.

In choosing a station, keep in mind that your selection should not be based on what *you* like to listen to, but on what your prospective buyers listen to. To whom do you want to advertise? Do you want to appeal to general interests or to some special interest?

If your community has only one station, its broadcasting range is probably limited. But you can be sure that a large percentage of the people of the community are listeners and that a large percentage of the listeners are local people. Even though you have no choice, this station may suit your advertising needs very well.

If more broadcasting stations are available, you will have to make a choice. This may not be as big a problem as you think, however. For various reasons, some stations will automatically be eliminated.

AM or FM RADIO?

The chief difference between the two is technical. AM broadcasts can be received over a wider area, but FM is static-free and has a better sound.

As the number of FM stations tripled over the past 15 years, programming on FM has evolved to the point that much of it is indistinguishable from AM. Nearly every American home now has at least one set capable of receiving FM. It is useful to remember, however, that not as many cars are equipped with radios that receive FM as are equipped with AM-only sets, although many car radios receive both. There is some movement toward a federal law requiring that alls sets priced above a certain level be able to receive both AM and FM.

VHF or UHF TELEVISION?

Again, as with radio, the differences are chiefly technical. VHF has the greater range and is less affected by obstructions.

Many of the currently operating UHF stations are located in heavily populated areas where all of the available VHF channels have been assigned. UHF stations often provide programming for segments of the community, such as Spanish-speaking viewers, who may find only limited attention paid to their interests on VHF stations.

WHO IS LISTENING, WATCHING?

The fact that it is technologically possible for people to tune in to a station does not mean that they do.

What you, the advertiser, should concern yourself about is how many sets are tuned to each station during specific time periods. You need to know what programs the people you want as customers listen to or watch. This information comes from surveys. If a station does not offer you at least one survey, ask for it.

Just as important as how many is who. Try to get demographic data (age, sex, income, educational level, etc.) for audiences of stations or programs to help you match a station to the customers you want.

SO WHICH STATION?

Radio stations characteristically enjoy high audience loyalty. Often a listener turns on the same station day after day and keeps it turned on most of the day. There is little switching. This loyalty factor is a consequence of the programming policy of the station. Programming policies determine the audience. Some programs appeal to general and diversified audiences; others are beamed to identifiable groups.

Most stations are strong on music, interspersed with newscasts, weather reports, and similar features. Each, however, is likely to feature a particular type of programming. Stations and programs may be categorized in several ways.

You will have a choice of middle-of-the-road music, all-news, rock, country-music, Spanish-language, soul, gospel, rhythm-and-blues, religious, farm, and classical-music stations. The whole range of people's interests and tastes finds expression on radio. The key to picking a station is, as always: Which audience do you want to advertise to? Who can use your product, service, or store?

In contrast to radio, television stations do not command strong audience loyalty. In television it is individual programs that attract audiences. Your aim in television advertising should be to get on or adjacent to the programs watched by the people you want as customers. These programs do not necessarily need to be the most popular ones—they just have to be the ones that your prospects are most likely to watch.

Stations often owe their popularity not just to program content, but to individual disc jockeys, newscasters, sportscasters, announcers, and other personalities.

If you find it hard to decide which of several stations to use, here is a possible solution. Advertise on one station for 13 weeks (or whatever period you choose), then switch to another station for the next 13 weeks, and so on. Eventually, you will return to the first station and start the cycle over again. In this way, you can advertise to all the people you want to reach.

PROGRAMS AND FEATURES

When you have selected a station, your next decision concerns how you will deliver your advertising message. You can choose between sponsoring your own program, sponsoring a station feature, and using spot announcements in a variety of ways.

Sponsored programs have the advantages of prestige and individual identification. Besides the syndicated programs, stations often have local-talent programs that can be sponsored. These programs usually have a strong local appeal.

Sponsored programs are not too common on radio. (Sponsored television programs are more common, of course, but usually they are at the national-advertiser level.) Unless a program is already on the air and has proved its popularity, you will have to build your own audience. Also, because of costs for both time and talent, you may feel that you must share the sponsorship. Most radio advertisers sponsor regular station features or use spot announcements. They can be more certain of their audiences.

Participating programs are usually owned by stations, which sell time on them for spot announcements. Advertisers on these programs are not identified as sponsors. Advertising on these programs may not help you build your image because you share them with other advertisers, but they may be good buys since they often have sizable audiences.

Sponsored features usually available are newscasts, weather and traffic reports, sports reviews, and market summaries. You might sponsor a feature every day or every other day.

SPOT ANNOUNCEMENTS

A spot is a commercial announcement lasting one minute or less. Spot announcements offer more flexibility than sponsored programs or features. You can vary the number of spots for different degrees of intensity and impact. You can concentrate them during certain hours to reach certain types of people or spread them throughout the day to reach a more varied audience. You can spread them among two or more stations to reach a larger number of people.

A *fixed spot* is contracted for and guaranteed to be broadcast at a time you choose. A *preemptible spot* is "semifixed": you pay a reduced rate for time you choose but risk being bumped by an advertiser willing to pay the higher fixed rate. You have little or no control over when a *floating spot* is broadcast; the station selects the broadcast time.

Spot announcements can be broadcast on participating programs, during station breaks between sponsored programs, run of station (ROS), or according to various package plans.

120

Run-of-station spots (ROS) are broadcast whenever time is available, as decided by the station. Those times may be during participating programs, but there is no guarantee that they will be. All your contract guarantees is that a certain number of spots will be broadcast during a stated period, such as a day or a week.

Package plans vary in name and exact composition with each station. They may include only run-of-station spots, or they may provide a certain number of spots in specified time classifications. Package plans are usually weekly, with a choice of one-minute or 30-second spots.

LENGTH OF SPOTS

Spot announcements may be one minute long, 30 seconds, 20 seconds, 10 seconds—sometimes even shorter. On radio about 80 percent run one minute; on television about 70 percent run 30 seconds. In a 10-second spot, about all you can do is identify yourself, announce what you are offering, and perhaps add a slogan. During a one-minute spot, you can also describe what you offer, state its benefits, and support your claims. Or you can advertise two items during a one-minute spot with less attention to each.

If radio is the only or the principal advertising medium you are going to use, one-minute spots are usually preferable. If it supplements other media, you may get good results from shorter spots.

HOW MANY SPOTS?

The number of spots and when and where they are placed will be governed to a great extent by how many advertising dollars you can spend. As a general rule, the more spots the better. One of the strong points of broadcast advertising is the opportunity for frequent repetition.

A plan often used is to follow a uniform basic schedule throughout the year, but to step up the number of spots for special promotions and during seasonal and holiday periods when buying is heavy.

Another effective technique is to advertise heavily for a period, then stop. This in-and-out advertising tactic is called a *flight*. It enables you to concentrate your broadcast advertisements for strong impact, while keeping your budget down from what it would be if you advertised continuously. For added impact, you can rotate your flights among several stations to reach different audiences.

WHAT DAYS OF THE WEEK?

Some advertisers find they get better response by concentrating their spot announcements on certain days of the week. Food stores do this on Thursdays, Fridays, and Saturdays. Others key their schedule to paydays in the community or to weekend shopping.

WHAT TIME OF DAY?

In general, radio is a daytime medium; nighttime belongs to television. Naturally, the periods sought by many advertisers are those with the greatest audience size and most desirable makeup— the period called *drive time* on radio, *prime time* on television.

Yet, other periods may have just the right audience for what you want to sell. Remember, you pay less for advertising time during the less-sought-after periods.

Not all people live on the same schedule. For example, radio is a companion for many night workers. Others watch old movies on TV into the early morning hours. An automobile dealer got a fine response in sales using late-night radio commercials. The manufacturer of a domestic-cleaning product bought spots during periods of the day and night for which there were few takers. His small business became capable of challenging well-known brands.

HOW RATES ARE QUOTED

Broadcast advertising-rate structures vary widely. Most rates are for spot announcements on: (1) participating programs, (2) special features, and (3) run of station (ROS), or the announcements are sold in packages. Rates are generally quoted for 60- and 30-second periods; some stations quote rates for 20 seconds or even less.

Rates are affected by the time of day the announcements will be broadcast. Rates are higher, of course, for periods most in demand.

For radio you may find day classifications such as AA, A, B, C, and D, with the highest rates paid for AA and the lowest for D. The hours are not exactly the same for all stations, but the following classification is typical:

Class AA, Morning drive time — 6 A.M. to 10 A.M.

Class B, Home worker time — 10 A.M. to 4 P.M.

Class A, Evening drive time — 4 P.M. to 7 P.M.

Class C, Evening time — 7 P.M. to 12 midnight

Class D, Night time — Midnight to 6 A.M.

Television stations may divide broadcast time similarly or, more likely, call their classifications daytime, early fringe, prime, late fringe, and weekend.

Each station seems to quote rates a little differently from every other station, but you can still compare rates by using the CPM (cost per thousand) formula. In general, you will find spot-announcement rates, participating-program spot-announcement rates, package rates, program rates, preemptible rates, and fixed-position rates. Fixed-position rates are the highest, since they guarantee that you will not be bumped from your position by another advertiser.

Advertising in all other time slots can be preempted. These slots can be recaptured by a station and sold to any advertiser willing to pay the fixed rate. Preemptible rates vary in proportion to the amount of notice that stations must give advertisers whose advertisements are being bumped. This notice can vary from two weeks to none.

If you are willing to take a chance that your announcements may be preempted with little notice, you can get good time buys on radio and television. If, however, you want to be sure your advertising reaches a large audience at a specific and much-desired time, you will have to pay higher rates.

No matter how many confusing rate-card variations may seem, they all boil down to one thing—they are prices for audiences. The time periods with the largest audiences command the highest rates. Yet, you may not need these large audiences. You may find that time slots with lower rates may include more of the people you want to attract as customers than the mass-appeal periods.

HOW TO SELECT ITEMS FOR RADIO ADVERTISING

Every merchandise category is a good candidate for radio advertising, but be sure to select the day part of your station carefully for each item to be sure the target audience is most concentrated on your station at that time.

Every price line can be a subject for radio spots. It was once thought that less-expensive merchandise sold better on radio. But it has been shown that men's suits, for instance, which are not a low-end item, sell very well on radio. Major applicances do too. Radio advertising attracts every income group.

A price leader might be considered a better choice than top-of-the-line for radio time when there is a sale, when it is imperative to get traffic into the store in order to sell a wide variety of merchandise, and as a tie-in with newspaper advertising.

HOW TO BUY TIME

Use at least ten 60-second spots over a *maximum* of three days to achieve good results with items on the air. This doesn't mean that ten whole spots are needed for each item advertised. Two items can often be sold in a 60-second spot, ten half-minute spots are enough. Try to combine items that are used together, are the same price, or are used by the same person.

Don't ask radio to do what newspaper ads can't do. Radio will not sell buyer's mistakes, out-of-season goods, or new and unfamiliar merchandise. One of radio's unique advantages is that it depends on the listener's ears and mental images. If a word doesn't conjure up a mental image, you have lost a prospect.

ENHANCE YOUR IMAGE

To attract the kind of customers (age, income, education, etc.) needed to keep pace with sales objectives, use radio to enhance what people in your market think about your store and to attract new customers. Radio can be used effectively to change the ideas that only younger/older people shop at your store, that your store hasn't kept up with fashion, that your store is good only for hard lines, or that your store sells cheap/expensive merchandise exclusively. Radio can be used also to announce that your store gives service, installation, or repair, or takes merchandise back and extends credit.

These are just a few of the preconceptions that can be changed with radio advertising. Through the use of varying devices, such as music, voices, humor, and sincerity, radio commercials can change what customers think of your business. Of course, projecting a new image on radio alone is not enough. All claims must be true.

SELL SERVICES

Radio is *especially* effective in selling services. Stores tend to become used to the services they offer and underplay or forget to mention them altogether. It is not easy to promote services in newspaper ads. They are often mentioned—not very effectively—in small print at the bottom of newspaper ads. Radio, on the other hand, can list them in the same tone of voice as the advertised item or event, and it can make the service pitch very affirmatively.

Service is a person-to-person thing. Radio can make the service point much more warmly and more decisively than newspapers. Some of the service areas which are effectively mentioned in radio commercials are:

► Parking

► Evening hours

► Credit plans

► Gift wrapping

► Delivery and pickup

► Appliance service

► Home-improvement planning

► Garden planning

► Public auditorium facilities for civic meetings

► Reliability

Spots for selling store services can be either separate, "all-service" commercials describing how friendly and helpful your people are, or a "liner" tagging another store commercial. Both approaches work well. The all-service commercial is particularly good in "rate-holder" situations. You can have several service commercials "standing" at the radio station and ask that they be aired when another item is cancelled.

CO-OP ADVERTISING (CO-OP)

Co-op advertising is an arrangement whereby advertising dollars are paid by the manufacturers of the goods to the retail seller of the goods. In other words, the people who make the products help the people who sell it by contributing to the advertising expenses. Over the years, the number of manufacturers and retailers involved in this type of advertising plan has grown rapidly. It permits the retailer to advertise his or her product and still make the same profit. Apprehensive business owners should always pump their vendors for possible co-op advertising support. It is important to let them know that the promotion of their items is as important as credit terms and delivery.

GETTING YOUR RADIO COMMERCIAL TOGETHER

Once you have made the decision to use radio, you must then construct the copy for the radio broadcast. Most of the time the radio station will do that for you. However, should you wish to do it yourself you will find the forms shown on the following pages helpful in preparing an appropriate spot announcement.

The Broadcast Announcement Worksheet (Table 7.1) is a simple planning device to help you select the proper format and subject matter. This sheet can be used to put your ideas into writing so that the radio station will have first-hand instructions from you.

TABLE 7.1
Broadcast
Announcement
Worksheet

COMPANY NAME:_____

POINT OF FOCUS FOR ANNOUNCEMENT:_____

_____

KEY POINTS OR FEATURES TO BE HIGHLIGHTED:_____

_____

_____

_____

TARGET AUDIENCE_____

LENGTH_____

COPY CONTENT:_____

_____

_____

_____

_____

_____

_____

_____

_____

_____

_____

_____

_____

_____

_____

_____

_____

_____

_____

SPECIAL INSTRUCTIONS:_____

_____

The second form is a Broadcast Copy Sheet (Table 7.2). It is from this type of sheet that the radio commercial is actually read at the station. By using this form you will be able to give precise instructions with your copy. It is a good idea to have a copy of what was actually broadcast.

**TABLE 7.2
Visual Broadcast
Worksheet
(Storyboard)**

FRAME #   OF   #

COMPANY NAME:_____

PRODUCT OR SERVICE TO BE
ADVERTISED:_____

_____

_____

KEY POINTS OR
FEATURES:_____

_____

_____

PICTURE OR
ILLUSTRATION:

VOCAL COPY:_____

_____

_____

_____

_____

_____

_____

SPECIAL INSTRUCTIONS:_____

_____

So as to eliminate the possibility of any error in communications it is best to place all orders for advertising in writing. Figures 7.1 and 7.2 are sample forms of a Broadcast order. Almost all radio stations will accept this order form. On this form you can spell out all the necessary in-

FIGURE 7.1

BROADCAST ORDER FORM

STATION: _____

CLIENT
ADVERTISER: _____

DATE

TIME	MON.	TUES.	WED.	THURS.	FRI.	SAT.	SUN.

TOTAL NUMBER
WEEKLY: _____

SPOT
LENGTH: _____

START DATE

TOTAL NUMBER
OF WEEKS: _____

INDIVIDUAL SPOT
COST: _____

TOTAL NUMBER
OF SPOTS: _____

TOTAL GROSS
COST: _____

END DATE

CANCELLATION
STATUS: _____

LESS AGENCY
COMMISSION: _____

NET PAY: _____

COPY

ENCLOSED PRINTED: _____

ENCLOSED CASSETTE: _____

ENCLOSED TAPE: _____

TO FOLLOW BY:

DATE
PICK UP AT:

NOTE: The Advertiser on this Contract is solely liable for the total amount of the advertising run against this Contract, until payment has been made to the Agency named on this Contract. Upon receipt of all monies towards this Contract the Agency shall become solely liable for all money due the media as per this Contract, less Agency commissions.

BILLING INSTRUCIONS:

AS AGENTS FOR THE ABOVE NAMED CLIENT, WE REQUEST
YOUR STATION TO BROADCAST THE ABOVE SCHEDULE.

SPECIAL INSTRUCTIONS

WE ACCEPT THE ABOVE ORDER AS STATED AND SHALL
BROADCAST THE ORDER ACCORDINGLY.

FIGURE 7.2

BROADCAST ORDER FORM

(SAMPLE)

CLIENT
ADVERTISER: ABC GENERAL STORE   STATION: KOOF Radio
1151 Maple St   6565 Boozer St.
Anytown, State 11111   12/10/79   Hitsville State 22222
                          DATE

TIME	MON.	TUES.	WED.	THURS.	FRI.	SAT.	SUN.
6am–9am	2	3	2	2	3	3	0
10am–Noon	1	2	1	1	2	2	0
Noon–7pm	3	5	5	2	6	0	0

TOTAL NUMBER
WEEKLY: 45   12/21/79   SPOT
                          START DATE   LENGTH: :60

TOTAL NUMBER
OF WEEKS: 4   INDIVIDUAL SPOT
                                            COST: 5.50

TOTAL NUMBER
OF SPOTS: 180   1/21/80   TOTAL GROSS
                          END DATE   COST: $ 990.00

CANCELLATION
STATUS: One week notice   LESS AGENCY
                                            COMMISSION: NONE

                                            NET PAY: $990.00

COPY

ENCLOSED PRINTED: Yes   NOTE: The Advertiser on this Contract is solely liable for the total amount of the
ENCLOSED CASSETTE: advertising run against this Contract, until payment has been made to the Agency
ENCLOSED TAPE: named on this Contract. Upon receipt of all monies towards this Contract the
TO FOLLOW BY: Agency shall become solely liable for all money due the media as per this Contract,
                             less Agency commissions.
         DATE
PICK UP AT:
ABC General

                             BILLING INSTRUCIONS: SEND INVOICE IN TRIPULCATE

                             AS AGENTS FOR THE ABOVE NAMED CLIENT, WE REQUEST
                             YOUR STATION TO BROADCAST THE ABOVE SCHEDULE.

                                            N/A

SPECIAL INSTRUCTIONS   WE ACCEPT THE ABOVE ORDER AS STATED AND SHALL
SEE ME FOR NEW COPY EVERY WK.   BROADCAST THE ORDER ACCORDINGLY.

**RADIO AND
TELEVISION**

FIGURE 7.3

Client _____

Start Date _____ End Date _____

Length _____ Live _____ Recorded _____

Product _____

Stations: _____ Co-op _____

Client Approval _____
Initial   Date

Producer _____

Client Requests: ☐ Duplicate Copy   ☐ Cassette   ☐ Reel to Reel   ☐ Air Check

SPECIAL
INSTRUCTIONS

10 Sec.

20 Sec.

30 Sec.

40 Sec.

50 Sec.

1 Min.

structions to ensure that your commercials air on time and in the proper sequence.

Figure 7.3 is an audio copy sheet. It is timed out in metered lines so as to aid in developing effective radio or television audio copy at precisely the correct length. Thus a reader can type out the desired copy to be read and at the same time measure its length.

8
WORD OF MOUTH — A MEDIUM ALL ITS OWN

Most intelligent business people know that one of the best forms of advertising is the "endless chain," or word-of-mouth advertising. This technique is a simple one: it means simply asking already-satisfied customers to refer their friends and neighbors to your business.

Many times in our complex mass-media-oriented society we tend to forget that the personal touch is many times the best. When was the last time you told a customer to bring or send in a friend? Quite a while? Never? Well, look at it this way: When a good customer asks someone to participate in your business, it implies that he or she is in fact endorsing your business, thus producing one of the best advertising campaigns at virtually no cost. In addition, you have made your customer feel important by including him or her in the success of your business.

If you are to have repeat business, you must give the customer a reason to come back to your store. Feeling important is one of those reasons. So get your customers involved in the promotion of the store. It is vital that businesspeople stay in close contact with their customers.

How do you get the names of others? Ask for them! There are several ways. Ask your customers if they know of anyone else who may be interested in the products and services that you carry. Explain that having their assistance is of the utmost importance to your business. Most of your customers feel, and rightfully so, that their buying decisions and actions carry weight with their friends and associates.

When is the best time to ask for new customers? Generally speaking, the best time is when your current customers have just made a satisfying purchase from your store: they are anxious to tell all their friends. When people ride an emotional high they want everyone else up there with them.

What's the best method for collecting new names?   One of the best proven methods is to give your current customers a card and ask them to fill out the information. You then have a good presold mailing list or direct (phone) response source. Your customers will sell your products, your services, your business—just give them a chance!

9
DIRECT MAIL
AND DIRECT
ADVERTISING

The difference between direct-mail advertising and its kin, direct advertising, is in the method of delivery. Direct-mail advertising is sent through the post office. Direct advertising is handed out by salespeople or distributed house to house. One or the other or both are used by almost every business, large or small. They may be your only advertising, or they may supplement advertising in other media.

They are the most selective and flexible of all media. They are *selective* because *you* decide who is to receive your advertising. You advertise only to people who can use what you sell. You can send your advertising to a few people or to many. You can confine it to a small area, such as a few city blocks, or distribute it throughout the entire United States. It is *flexible* because the sizes and shapes of your ad are pretty much up to you. The presentation can be simple or elaborate. You distribute it when you choose—you are independent of publication dates and broadcast schedules. You are in control all the time.

Another advantage is that the readers are not distracted by other advertising. For a moment, at least, you have their undivided attention. At the same time, however, you have no editorial or entertainment support to keep readers exposed to your advertising. Direct-mail advertising has to be good, both in what it offers and in how the offer is presented in words and pictures. The same is true of direct advertising.

USES OF DIRECT-MAIL ADVERTISING Direct-mail advertising has many uses for manufacturers, retailers, and service businesses. Here are a few of them:

► To solicit mail-order or phone-order business.

134

► To presell prospects before a sales call—to soften up the buyer by acquainting him or her with your company and your products.

► To announce new models, new designs, new lines, new items, or changes in your products, services, or equipment.

► To notify your customers of price increases or decreases.

► To substitute for a sales call on a regular customer.

► To follow up on sales calls to prospects.

► To welcome new customers.

► To help regain lost customers.

► To increase the full-line selling of your salesforce.

► To thank all customers for their business at least once a year.

► To create an image for your business.

► To remind customers and prospects of seasonal or periodic needs.

► To make the most of special events such as feature sales.

► To take advantage of printed advertising materials supplied by manufacturers.

If you doubt that you are reaching all customers and prospects through other advertising media, direct mail gives you another chance. If you are already reaching them, direct mail adds to the impact.

KEEPING YOUR MAILING LIST UP TO DATE

The list that you build yourself is undoubtedly a good list in many ways because you selected the names yourself. But are you sure that it is correct and up to date?

This is one of the greatest problems in direct-mail advertising. As many as 25 percent of the entries on a mailing list may change in some way during a single year. People die, move, are promoted, change employers, or retire. Companies go out of business, merge, or make other changes.

Is each name on your list spelled correctly? Are the initials right? Is the address still correct? If not, what is the new address? Can you still expect to do business with the addressee there, or is the new location too far away? If the addressee is a businessperson, is he or she still with the same company? Is his or her title still the same? His or her location?

WHAT YOU CAN DO ABOUT IT

First of all, no matter how small or how large your mailing list is, make one person responsible for changes. If everyone looks after the list, it will either be neglected or become disorganized.

Here are some other steps you can take to keep your list current:

- ► Be sure that all changes in your accounts receivable are made in the mailing lists.

- ► If the names are from sources such as telephone books and trade directories, check your list every time a new issue of the source comes out.

- ► Watch newspapers, business papers, and other media where deaths, promotions, and moves to different companies are reported.

- ► Require your salesforce to report personnel changes in customer companies, preferably in writing.

- ► Periodically—perhaps once a year—send to each name on the list a double postcard, one half asking if the address is correct and the other half a postage-guaranteed return postcard for the reply.

HELP FROM THE POST OFFICE

On third-class mail, you can print on the envelope "Address Correction Requested." A small fee is collected for each undelivered piece when the information—reason for nondelivery or addressee's new address—is delivered to you. If your mailing piece weighs more than six ounces and you wish to have it returned with the information, it must carry the words "Address Correction Requested. Return Postage Guaranteed." In this case, the return postage will be added to the fee. Return of smaller pieces are included in the fee.

In addition, take your mailing list (on cards) to the Post Office periodically, and ask that the addresses be checked. You will have to pay a small charge, but the money you save in postage and other mailing costs will more than make up for the charge. Furthermore, your mailings will be more efficient.

THE COST OF DIRECT-MAIL ADVERTISING

Direct mail is the most costly advertising medium in terms of dollars spent versus size of audience or readership. But because of the high percentage of returns, it can be one of the cheapest in terms of results. The true measure of the cost of advertising is the *cost per inquiry or per sale*.

You can get some idea of what a mailing will cost by estimating the following elements and totaling them. Make your estimates on a per-piece basis.

► The cost of preparing the folder or other literature to be enclosed, if any.

► The cost of processing a letter.

► The cost of the envelope.

► The cost of addressing the envelope, inserting the enclosures, and sealing.

► The postage, either first or third class.

Table 9.1 shows a more detailed estimating form. To keep track of returns from a mailing, the reply card or envelope of each mailing should be coded.

DIRECT ADVERTISING

Some direct advertising is distributed in the course of personal selling. When salespeople call on customers or prospects, they usually leave catalog pages, specification sheets, folders, and other sales literature. Or the customer may pick it up at your place of business.

If direct-advertising pieces such as handbills, flyers, or throwaways are to be distributed house to house, someone has to do the legwork. You can turn the job over to a company that specializes in this work, or you can hire individual workers to do the job. If you hire the workers

**TABLE 9.1
Direct Mail
Campaign Budget
for One Mailing**

NAME OF MAIL PIECE: _____   CLIENT: _____

OBJECTIVE: _____   PREPARED BY: ____   DATE: ____

A. DIRECT EXPENSES

   1. Planning/Administrative/
      Operating Salaries (Work
      Hours x Hourly Rate) _____

   2. Creative Costs/Preparations
      a. Copy _____
      b. Layout _____
      c. Artwork _____
      d. Photography/Retouching _____
      e. Printing Preparation _____ _____

   3. Printing/Paper/Materials _____

   4. Other Enclosures _____

   5. Envelopes/Wrappers _____

   6. Mailing List Rental/Purchase _____

   7. Mailing List Maintenance _____

   8. Mailing Piece Preparation
      (folding, inserting, labeling,
      addressing, etc.) _____

   9. Postage _____
      a. Outgoing _____
      b. Return _____ _____

  10. If Selling Merchandise
      a. Cost of Merchandise _____
      b. Packaging _____
      c. Handling _____
      d. Postage/Shipping _____
      e. Royalties _____
      f. Refunds/Cancellations _____
      g. Refurbish Returns _____
      h. Bad Debts _____
      i. Storage _____ _____

  11. Other _____

TOTAL DIRECT EXPENSES _____

TABLE 9.1 (Cont.) B. ALLOCATION OF OVERHEAD
EXPENSES
1. Office Space   _____
2. Office Supplies   _____
3. Utilities   _____
4. Maintenance   _____
5. Salaries   _____
6. Travel   _____
7. Accounting   _____
8. Taxes, Licenses   _____
9. Other   _____
TOTAL OVERHEAD EXPENSES   _____

C. TOTAL CAMPAIGN BUDGET
(A + B)   _____

D. PLUS 5–15% FOR TESTING   _____

E. ADJUSTED TOTAL CAMPAIGN
BUDGET (C + D)   _____

yourself, you or somebody else will have to organize and supervise the distribution.

It is illegal to have your direct-advertising pieces put in mailboxes, since you have not paid postage on them. You must make sure that they are put in some other secure place—tucked neatly alongside doorknobs or under doors. If they blow away, they will not reach the persons for whom they are intended, and the litter they create can hurt your reputation.

10
YOUR ADVERTISING BUDGET

When your advertising budget is finished, it will consist mostly of figures. Yet it is really a plan to be used for checking progress. Your expenditures will mark the completion of parts of the plan.

"How much should I spend for advertising?" is a question often asked. And often the answer, even if it satisfies the asker, is far from the best solution.

There are five possible approaches to deciding how much to spend for advertising:

► Spending "all we can afford"

► Allotting a certain percent of sales

► Trying to match the advertising of competitors

► Investing for future profits

► The objective-and-task method

THE "ALL-WE-CAN-AFFORD" APPROACH This approach treats advertising as a luxury. It is a financial rather than a marketing approach. It does not even consider what advertising can or should accomplish.

THE PERCENT-OF-SALES APPROACH The "all-we-can-afford" approach is more or less arbitrary. Most people want a formula—for instance, a certain percent of past sales (usually the previous year) or of estimated sales for the budgeting period. But any formula raises two questions: "Is this formula right?" and "Is it right for *me*?"

140

The percent-of-sales approach to advertising is used more often than any other method. It is simple and easy to use, and it gives the user a sense of security. But it has some weaknesses.

Using the previous year's sales as a base seems to suggest that advertising is the result of sales rather than sales the result of advertising. Furthermore, it is not forward looking. It makes no provision for increasing business, and may not even allow enough money to maintain the current level of advertising. With rising costs, more dollars might be needed to buy the same amount of space or time.

Using the sales forecast for the budgeting period as a base at least recognizes advertising's contribution to the selling effort. A danger here is that the forecast may be too optimistic. If sales do not come up to expectations, a cutback is likely to be made. Then, when advertising is needed even more than before, no advertising funds, or at best fewer, are available.

Another danger in the percent-of-sales method is that you may rely too much on figures found in business and government publications. These figures are useful to a degree, but they are averages based on the expenditures of both small and large advertisers. They may not be right for you.

What percent to use, if you use this method, depends on a number of factors. If you are competing against a larger company with a correspondingly larger advertising budget, you may need to use a larger percent, even though you cannot match the larger firm dollar for dollar. If you are introducing a new or improved product, if you are opening a new store or a new department in your present store, if you are trying to expand your business in any way whatsoever, you have to put forth an extra effort. This usually calls for more advertising, at least at the start.

A variation of the percentage approach is the *unit-of-sales method.* This method establishes the amount of advertising on the basis of unit quantities of goods instead of dollar sales.

MATCHING COMPETITION

Trying to match the advertising of your competitors is a defensive approach. It tends to result in blind imitation rather than careful analysis of your own needs.

ADVERTISING AS AN INVESTMENT

The approach that considers advertising an investment for future profits is forward looking, but it is also risky. It is used mainly for introducing new products or other new enterprises.

At first, expenditures exceed sales income. Any possible profits are plowed back into advertising and other promotional and sales activities. Eventually, income must cover all costs, including advertising, and yield a profit. This may take a year or longer.

THE OBJECTIVE-AND-TASK METHOD To plan an advertising budget properly you must think about what you expect your advertising to accomplish. An increase in total sales volume? Higher sales in a specific department? More sales of certain models or lines of equipment? Some other objective?

With the budgeting methods described above, you start by determining the total amount of money available for advertising. Then you break down the lump sum according to when and how it will be spent.

With the objective-and-task method, you build up your budget by first deciding what advertising you need and then determining the various costs involved. Most advertising specialists agree that this is the best method.

In using the objective-and-task method, you should state your objectives in specific rather than general terms. Objectives such as "maintaining present business," "increasing sales to present customers," or "getting new customers" are too general. Instead of just trying to "increase sales," specify in your objective that you are going to increase overall sales by increasing sales of a particular line of products or certain models. The new customers you aim to bring in could be buyers in a particular industry, people in a certain community, or people in a specific age group, such as teenagers or young married couples.

If your objective is to attract new customers, you may already be advertising in newspapers and decide that you could also reach these potential new customers with radio advertising. In that case, you might cut down on your newspaper advertising and divert some money to radio. Or you could maintain the same volume of newspaper advertising and increase your budget to add radio advertising. If you advertise in business papers of one or more industries, you might add papers in other industries to locate new customers.

The principal problem in using the objective-and-task method is that it is easy to become overly ambitious. When your figures are totaled, you may find that the cost is more than you can possibly afford, no matter how much you want to be forward looking and aggressive. The solution is usually to revise your objectives and/or modify your plans

142

for achieving them along more realistic lines. Your revised program can still be a good one.

PUTTING YOUR BUDGET ON PAPER

When you have decided how much to spend on advertising, you are ready to distribute the amount by months and by media. Use an accounting sheet or a form you have ruled off. Across the top, list the months; on the left side, list the media you intend to use.

If your budget is simple, you may be able to get everything on this one sheet. More likely, you will need a master sheet with supporting sheets. The master sheet shows how much you intend to spend each month for advertising in each medium—newspapers, radio, business papers, direct mail, and so on. The supporting sheet for newspapers, for example, will show under each month the publication, date, and size of insertion for each advertisement. Similar sheets are prepared for radio, business papers, or whatever other media you plan to use. If you are a manufacturer, you may also want your budget broken down by products; if a retailer, by departments.

The amounts budgeted need not be the same for all months of the year. A manufacturer advertising in business papers is likely to have a fairly uniform budget, but a retailer will probably vary the amount from month to month because of holiday, seasonal, and other special promotions.

Do not forget that advertising costs include preparation of the advertisement as well as space or time. Even if you get free help from the medium, such as copy and layout for your advertisements, you will probably have to pay for engravings and other materials.

A common practice in business-paper advertising is to prepare a series of advertisments and then rotate them throughout the year. For media such as newspapers and radio, more new advertisements are likely to be needed through the year. Include estimated preparation costs in your budget in the months when you are most likely to make changes. Also, you should have a reserve for taking care of advertising opportunities you can't foresee.

Do not think that the budget you finally put on paper is the last word. You will need to review it periodically for whatever changes seem necessary. Most budgets are revised after six months, but there may be good reason for quarterly or even more frequent reviews. Keep track of your estimates and expenditures. Forms such as the ones shown in Tables 10.1 and 10.2 can be very useful.

TABLE 10.1
Budget and
Expenditures
Control Sheet
for 19 _____.

MONTH	BUDGET	ACTUAL	VARIANCE	COMMENTS
January				
February				
March				
April				
May				
June				
July				
August				
September				
October				
November				
December				
	TOTAL YR BUDGET	TOTAL YR ACTUAL	TOTAL YR VARIANCE	

HOW TO STRETCH YOUR ADVERTISING DOLLARS

Regardless of how small or how big your advertising budget is, you naturally want to get the greatest possible return for your money. At the same time, there are situations in which an advertising expenditure that might seem extravagant will make your dollars more productive and more than pay for itself.

Repeating advertisements is one way to make advertising dollars go farther. You save on preparation costs, both creative and mechanical. Some businesses must change their advertisements often

144

PERIOD FROM   TO

TABLE 10.2
Media Schedule
Control

	Size or length	Dates to run	Product or dept featured	Cost	Remarks
Media Circulation Rate Closing Date Dates of Contract					
Media Circulation Rate Closing Date Dates of Contract					
Media Circulation Rate Closing Date Dates of Contract					
Media Circulation Rate Closing Date Dates of Contract					
Media Circulation Rate Closing Date Dates of Contract					

because special offerings are their lifeblood, but this is not the case for industrial advertisers nor for some local businesses. A number of studies have shown that advertisements repeated as many as four times do not lose their effectiveness. A later insertion attracts about the same number of readers as the first one.

Local firms that emphasize service day in and day out do not need to change their advertisements often because what they sell does not change often. Banks and other financial services, repair shops, fuel dealers, and eating establishments are examples of this.

Another way to get extra mileage from your advertising dollars is to convert publication advertisements to direct-mail pieces. This is especially helpful when you have gone to the expense of obtaining color plates. You already have an investment in copy, layout, art, and mechanical preparation. With a little revision, you will have a direct-mail piece for less than what an entirely new one would cost. Or you can reprint the advertisement without change and use it either as an attachment to a letter or, if it is reprinted on heavier paper, as a self-mailer.

COLOR—IS IT WORTH THE COST?

Color adds to the cost of an advertisement. The rates charged by media are higher than for black and white, and the mechanical preparation also costs more. In addition to the black plates, a separate plate is required for each primary color used. For many purposes, black-and-white advertisements are entirely satisfactory, but sometimes color is worth the extra cost.

Color has always been used to get attention, though in a publication with many color pages a well-done black-and-white advertisement may attract attention because of the contrast. For foods, clothing, and other products where color influences buying, there is no doubt that color increases the effectiveness of advertisements. Also, a color background can create atmosphere and contribute to the emotional appeal.

11
COPYWRITING

Once you have purchased radio time, you must then write the commercial itself. This is known as "COPY."

Many larger stations and some smaller stations have copywriters, people who write copy for the sales staff. But because some stations require that you write your own copy, you should learn to write good copy.

Remember that the words you write must tell a complete story in a very short period of time. The story must be written simply so it can be understood by people who cannot see the printed words.

A good rule to remember is that each piece of copy must answer the following questions:

WHO

WHAT

WHERE

WHEN

sometimes even   WHY

Make the information as clear and concise as possible. You are trying to inform and excite with your commercial. If you confuse the audience, you will defeat your own purpose.

As you well know and customers seem to sense, COPY is the most important factor in how well radio—or any other medium—works for you.

Here are some tips for copywriters:

1. *Know what you are writing about.* Use whatever fact sheets you have from the manufacturer, spend time on the floor

learning what customers look at and ask for in specific merchandise. Keep up to date on new products, new fibers, and new ways of doing things.

2. *Talk about customer benefits.* Remember what the customers are concerned about. "What's in it for me?" Then talk directly to them, tell them what the item will do for their convenience, happiness, family, etc.

3. *Use action words.* "Get to the Big Store sale today" is much better than "There's a big sale at Mark's Sporting Goods Store today." Action words motivate listeners to think about getting down to the store.

4. *Mention your name as many times as you can.* This will inform those who tune in after the commercial is underway.

5. *Use short, punchy sentences* that are easy to understand.

6. *Pitch copy to the prime target.* Decide who is most likely to buy the item and talk directly to that customer—nobody else.

7. *Watch out for superlatives.* They weaken your story when they are hard to believe. Stick to benefits and news.

8. *Don't die at the end.* Some commercials start out strong, then run downhill as though the writer had lost interest in the project. *Build and hold.*

9. *Read the script out loud to yourself.* This is a most important rule. Does copy flow? Are there any tongue-twisters? Radio writing is for the ear alone. It should not be poetic, but clear and easily understood.

Particularly in industrial advertising, color can sometimes provide a better understanding of the product. For example, color can focus attention on particular parts of a complicated apparatus or illustrate more clearly an operation such as the flow of a liquid or gas.

ABOUT TYPE

Newspapers, most business papers, and some consumer magazines will set your advertisements in type without charge. Sometimes, however, it is better to pay a shop that specializes in typesetting to do the job. Such a shop usually offers a wide selection of typefaces (designs) and sizes. Publications often have only a limited selection.

If all you are interested in is communicating facts, you may believe that the appearance of the advertisement does not matter very much. But type does more than merely convey information. It creates an image, an atmosphere, for your business. Be sure it creates the image you want.

Large, heavy type used in a store advertisement, for instance, shouts low prices. The same type, used for advertising such products as machinery, can suggest ruggedness. For advertising dresses and other merchandise for women, a light, graceful type suggests femininity. If an advertisement is not crowded with type, the white space can suggest quality.

12
COOPERATIVE ADVERTISING

Cooperative advertising accounts for one dollar of every six dollars spent for local advertising, according to one estimate. Exact figures are impossible to compile because much of the information is confidential, but many consumer products and some industrial products can be advertised under a cooperative plan.

WHAT IS COOPERATIVE ADVERTISING?

In theory, cooperative advertising is this: Manufacturers advertise brand-name products nationally to persuade people *what* to buy. To tell people *where* to buy, they may offer to share with retailers the cost of local advertising.

By using this system the manufacturer gets more advertising per dollar because the local rates a retailer pays for advertising space are lower than the national rates a manufacturer must pay. For the retailer, cooperative advertising is an incentive to stock and advertise brand-name products.

Cooperative-advertising plans differ according to the different manufacturers. The conditions of some plans can be explained on a single typewritten sheet; others are so complicated that it may take 12 or more printed sheets or pages to describe them. But any plan is certain to include the points discussed below.

LENGTH OF TIME COVERED

Partly because of annual changes in models, styles, and so on, and partly because of accounting practices, many cooperative-advertising plans are drawn up for one year. Occasionally, they may be for a longer period. For special promotions, plans may specify shorter periods.

COST SHARING

The most common ratio for sharing costs is 50-50, but other ratios are sometimes used. Some plans provide for cost sharing not only by the manufacturer but also by distributors or wholesalers.

FUNDS

Manufacturers set aside cooperative funds for the dealer according to a stated percent of dollar purchases or amount per unit of purchase. The amount accumulated in this fund sets the dollar limit on the manufacturer's share for that dealer.

MEDIA

The cooperative-advertising plan specifies what media the retailer may use and the conditions of its use. Newspapers are almost certain to be acceptable; they get about 70 percent of all cooperative-advertising dollars. Other media are usually permitted, as well, in order to make the plan more flexible, especially for small dealers.

PROOF OF PERFORMANCE

To be reimbursed from a cooperative fund, the dealer must present proof of advertising and a copy of the receipted invoice. For newspaper advertising, a tearsheet of the page on which the advertisement appeared is required.

For radio or TV, proof is a certified copy of the script listing rates, the number of times the advertisement was broadcast, and when it was broadcast. To speed up approvals and reduce delays in reimbursement for broadcast cooperative advertising a standard procedure and form, the "radio tearsheet," is now being used.

For outdoor advertising, a photograph of one of the mounted posters or painted bulletins is required along with details of display locations and dates.

These are the essentials, but there may be other requirements; for instance, illustrations, brand-name logotypes, or wording may be either required or prohibited.

HOW COOPERATIVE ADVERTISING WORKS

After a retailer has run an advertisement eligible for cooperative-advertising funds, the retailer pays the medium for the total cost. Then he or she forwards the receipted invoice and the required proof of performance to the manufacturer, requesting reimbursement. Reimbursment is either by check or by credit memorandum.

Suppose, for example, that you buy $2,000 worth of merchandise from a company and make a cooperative-advertising agreement which provides that that company will put 2 percent of purchases into the fund and share the costs 50-50. At the time of purchase, the manufacturer credits $40 to your cooperative-advertising account.

Now suppose that you advertise the manufacturer's product at a cost of $60. You pay the $60 and request reimbursement as explained above. When your request is approved, you get back $30.

You now have a balance of $10 in your cooperative-advertising fund to apply to future advertising. But by the time you advertise this product again, you will probably have made other purchases from the manufacturer, and your cooperative-advertising fund will have built up again.

There are many complaints about cooperative funds. Retailers, both large and small, complain about restrictions on use of the funds and about their administration by the manufacturers. Manufacturers charge abuses by retailers.

Since cooperative advertising comes within the Robinson-Patman Act, it is regulated by the Federal Trade Commission. Whether you are a retailer or a manufacturer, you should get a copy of the Guide put out by the FTC explaining in simple language the legal problems involved in advertising allowances.

RETAILERS AND COOPERATIVE ADVERTISING

Some retailers do not use cooperative-advertising plans at all. Others do not advertise up to the limit of the cooperative funds they are entitled to use. Perhaps you are not getting as much from cooperative advertising as you might.

YOU HAVE PAID FOR IT

If you are a retailer, perhaps you have not done much cooperative advertising because you do not want to spend your own money in order to collect what is often spoken of as the "factory share." However, the factory share is already included in the price you pay for whatever you purchase from the manufacturer. If you want to get back what you have in effect already paid into the fund, you have to advertise.

Unspent cooperative money retained by a manufacturer often becomes part of the profits. Even so, sales and advertising executives would prefer that all cooperative advertising funds be spent for advertising. The purpose of the advertising is to help increase product sales, which, in turn, will bring even greater profits.

152

STORE
TRAFFIC

If you are selling brand-name products that have strong national advertising support, telling people that they can buy those products at your store can increase store traffic for sales of other merchandise. Many manufacturers announce their national advertising schedules to dealers in advance so that stores carrying their products can get maximum results from local advertising by adapting it to the manufacturers' schedules.

CHOICE OF
MEDIA

In their cooperative-advertising plans, manufacturers state which media they favor. Paid-circulation newspapers, both dailies and weeklies, especially when circulations are audited, are almost always approved. Policies vary on nonpaid suburban newspapers and shoppers. They often are treated as exceptions. The trend seems to be to approve suburban newspapers with audited circulations. Shoppers are seldom acceptable. Other usually favored media include radio, television, outdoor, and transit.

You may find that it is not practical to use any of the media listed in a cooperative-advertising plan, such as newspapers or radio, because the amounts of money accrued are too small or because these media reach beyond limited sales areas. In such cases, the Federal Trade Commission requires manufacturers to offer "functionally available" alternative media. Examples cited by the FTC are envelope stuffers and handbills.

If you believe that you are too restricted under any plan, you should ask for an exception or special consideration. But be prepared to back up your request with facts. You must show that you have made a careful analysis of the situation, including all available media.

You must also be sure that your request conforms to the provisions of the Robinson-Patman Act. Under cetain conditions, the retailer may be guilty along with the manufacturer when there is a violation of the act.

UP-TO-DATE
RECORDS
ARE
ESSENTIAL

If you are going to get the most out of cooperative advertising, whether alone or jointly with other retailers, you need to keep detailed, up-to-date records.

Be sure you have the latest copy of the cooperative-advertising plan for every manufacturer whose products you sell. If you are missing any, ask your wholesaler (if you buy from a wholesaler) or the manufacturer's representative (if you buy direct). If you write to a manufacturer, be sure to identify yourself positively as selling that company's products.

For each manufacturer or product, set up a separate record. Basic information should include:

► Effective dates of the plans (including latest date for submitting reimbursement claims).

► Ratio of cost sharing (50-50 or whatever it is).

► How credits accrue (percent of purchases or so much per unit).

► How to submit claims (proof of performance, etc.).

► Other manufacturer requirements.

The first item is particularly important. If you are not alert to the last date on which you can submit your claim for reimbursement, you will probably lose money. Manufacturers customarily allow 30, 60, or 90 days after a plan ends for customers to get their claims in. After this period, no claims are paid.

Whenever you receive a delivery from a manufacturer, enter on the record how much cooperative-advertising money you have earned. Also, make entries when you submit claims for reimbursement and when the claims are paid. At all times, you should know how much uncommitted cooperative funds you have with each manufacturer.

The best plan is to do your cooperative advertising throughout the year when you can benefit most. As you approach the date when a plan runs out, review how you stand with the manufacturer. Maybe you can still do some cooperative advertising that will bring additional sales and more profits. That is better than allowing the funds to revert to the manufacturer because you did not use them.

Be very organized in your approach to cooperative advertising. The forms shown in Figs. 12.1-12.3 could be very useful to you.

GROUP POOLING OF MONEY

If you are a retailer with few cooperative dollars available from each manufacturer whose products you sell, group advertising can get you more for every dollar. By pooling your money with other small retailers selling the same products, you can buy larger space in print media or more spot announcements on broad-

FIGURE 12.1

Co-op advertising information request

_____ Date

Manufacturer's Name _____

Home Office Address _____

I am budgeting a yearly advertising program for my store. In order to take advantage of any Co-op Advertising allowances offered by vendors supplying me, I would appreciate your filling out the following information and returning it to me by _____ Date

Thank you for your help.

Cordially, _____

1. Does your company offer a co-op ad allowance that I qualify for? YES _____ NO _____

2. If answer to question #1 is YES, and your company has a printed Co-op Program, simply send the program and answer only those questions *not* covered in your printed plan. If NO, please return the entire form to me in the enclosed envelope.

3. What is the basis of accrual of co-op funds? (Example: 3% of net purchases, 5% of net purchases, open end or 50¢ per unit, etc.)
_____
_____

4. What is the time period, that the accrual is based on? (Example: based on last calendar year's purchases)
_____
_____

5. How much ad allowances, based on my purchases, have I available to spend?
   Dollar figure: _____

6. Please stipulate whether your Co-op Program is on a 50/50 — 75/25 — 100% paid, or a fixed line rate basis.
_____
_____

7. What are the time limits in which the Co-op ads must appear in the paper, to insure your company's participation?
_____
_____

8. What "proof of performance" does your co-op plan require? (Example: tear sheet, newspaper invoice, store invoice, etc.)
_____
_____

9. How soon after an ad appears must we submit "proof of performance" to your company and whom do we mail it to in order to get paid?
_____
_____

10. What requirements does your company have in order for us to comply with their co-op plan. (Example: ads must use illustrations of product, registry symbols, product logo, etc.)
_____
_____

11. Are there any restrictions in your co-op plan regarding newspaper classified advertising?
_____
_____

If your company has a printed Co-Op Plan and/or retail advertising kit, will you please enclose it with this form and mail to me today.

This form has been completed by

_____ Name

_____ Title

_____ Phone

_____ Retailer authorized signature

155

FIGURE 12.2

gather co-op program information using a form like this

**COOPERATIVE
ADVERTISING**

Co-op advertising information request

Manufacturer's Name _____ February 1, 1978 _____
Home Office Address
Date

Nordstrom Manufacturing Co.
1435 Sanders St.
Bell City, Ohio O6512
Attn. National Sales Manager

I am budgeting a yearly advertising program for my store. In order to take advantage of any Co-op Advertising allowances offered by vendors supplying me, I would appreciate your filling out the following information and returning it to me by **March 15, 1978**

Date

Thank you for your help

Cordially, _____ Frank W. Wilson _____
Frank's Appliance Store
Lebanon, Missouri 6/202

1. Does your company offer a co-op ad allowance that I qualify for? YES X NO ___

2. If answer to question #1 is YES, and your company has a printed Co-op Program, simply send the program and answer only those questions not covered in your printed plan. If NC, please return the entire form to me in the enclosed envelope

3. What is the basis of accrual of co-op funds? (Example: 3% of net purchases, 5% of net purchases, unlimited, or 50¢ per unit, etc.)

_____ 10% of your purchases _____

4. What is the time period that the accrual is based on? (Example: based on last calendar year's purchases)

_____ This year's purchases _____

5. How much ad allowances, based on my purchases, have I available to spend?

Dollar figure: _____ $1,500.00 _____

6. Please stipulate whether your Co-op Program is on a 50/50 — 75/25 — 100% paid, or a fixed line rate basis

_____ 100% paid _____

7. What are the time limits in which the Co-op ads must appear in the paper to insure your company's participation?

_____ March 1st thru August 31st _____

8. What "proof of performance" does your co-op plan require? (Example: tear sheet, newspaper invoice, store invoice, etc.)

_____ A tear sheet and duplicate net invoice from your newspaper _____

9. How soon after an ad appears must we submit "proof of performance" to your company and whom do we mail it to in order to get paid?

_____ 30 Days _____
Attn. Co-op Auditing Dept. - Nordstrom Mfg. Co.
1435 Sanders St., Bell City, Ohio O65/2

10. What requirements does your company have in order for us to comply with their co-op plan (Example: ads must use illustrations of product, registry symbols, product logo, (your policy on competing products in same ad, etc.)

_____ Logo and trademark - a picture _____

11. Are there any restrictions in your co-op plan regarding newspaper classified advertising?

_____ No! As long as a picture of our product and our logo appear in the newspaper ad _____

If your company has a printed Co-Op Plan and/or retail advertising kit, will you please enclose it with this form and mail to me today.

This form has been completed by _____ Thomas C. Nordstrom _____
Name
_____ National Sales Mgr. _____
Title
_____ 614-222-3156 _____
Phone

_____ Frank W. Wilson _____
Retailer authorized signature

156

© Newspaper Advertising Bureau

collect co-op money using a form like this

FIGURE 12.3

Cooperative advertising claim

TO: *Co-op Auditing Dept.*
Nordstrom Manufacturing Co.
1435 Sanders St.
Bell City, Ohio 06512

FROM: *Frank's Appliance Store*
185 Madison St.
Lebanon, Missouri
61202

We submit the following cooperative advertising claim in accordance with the terms of your cooperative advertising program. Proof of advertising is enclosed in the form of duplicate bills and newspaper tear sheets.

Your prompt issuance of a credit or a check covering payment of this claim is expected and will enable us to continue and extend use of your cooperative advertising program.

Newspaper	Date of Advertisement	Space Used	Net Rate	Total Cost	Vendor's Co-op Cost
Lebanon Daily Record	*April 15, 1978*	*80 inches*	*$5.00 per inch*	*$400.00*	*$400.00*

I certify that the above is billed at my exact LOWEST NET RATE, computed after all normally earned discounts and expected rebates—and that the amount billed does not include (1) production costs, (2) special or preferred position premiums. If any further discounts or rebates, other than those already computed, are earned by us for space used, your share will be promptly refunded.

Date *May 3, 1978*

Signature *Frank W. Wilson*

cast media. The impact on readers and listeners can be just as great as that of a large retailer advertising alone. Moreover, you can buy space or time at lower rates. The combined funds of the group might even be sufficient to permit you to use color.

Attitudes of media toward group or multiple-signature advertisements are changing. At one time advertisements with two or more names listed were charged at the higher national rates and the lower local rates were charged when only one name appeared. Now, more and more media are offering group or cooperative rates, which fall between national and local rates, to encourage more cooperative advertising.

A question arises about how much each individual retailer will or will not benefit. A fear of competition is understandable, but you are not likely to lose sales to other dealers whose names appear in the same advertising. Often, participating retailers are not located close to each other. Even if some in the group are close enough to be competitive, people are just as likely to buy from you as from any of the others. Furthermore, people are likely to buy from one retailer instead of another for reasons other than locations.

MANUFACTURERS AND COOPERATIVE ADVERTISING

If you are a manufacturer, you may be facing either of two questions: If you have a cooperative plan, should you continue it? If not, should you start one?

Cooperative advertising can cause plenty of headaches for the manufacturer. This is true no matter how detailed your plan is. Some companies have had a plan in operation and discontinued it. Others have stopped and then gone back to it because of pressures from retailers or because of their competitors' plans. You may feel forced into cooperative advertising.

REASONS FOR AND AGAINST

The two principal reasons advanced for offering cooperative advertising are (1) that you get more advertising for your dollars because of the lower local rates paid by the retailer, and (2) that you have something to offer that will attract dealers.

A prime reason for *not* going into cooperative advertising is the amount of work required for administration of the plan—keeping a record of the credits and disbursements in each retailer's fund, checking performance with invoices, carrying on correspondence when a retailer fails to comply with the rules. Also, enforcement of the plan sometimes puts a strain on relations with a dealer because the dealer fails, intentionally or unintentionally, to comply with the provisions of the plan.

Finally, you have little real control over how cooperative advertising fits into your own marketing plan. Because funds are built up by purchases, most cooperative-advertising money is likely to be used in markets where you need its help the least.

BEFORE YOU START

If you are thinking about getting into cooperative advertising, do more than read or simply model a plan after the plans of other companies. Consult someone with experience in all the ins and outs of cooperative advertising. No one will be able to tell you how to forestall all trouble, but if you consult others you can probably hold it to a minimum.

13
MEASURING THE RESULTS OF ADVERTISING

If you are new to the retail or service business, you may still be learning about advertising through trial and error. Perhaps you watch your competitors and run ads when they do. Or you run an ad only when you can offer a bargain.

Whether you are a newcomer or a veteran advertiser, you should always keep one question foremost in your thinking: How much good is my advertising doing?

In a small firm, neither time nor money is sufficient to engage in complicated ad-measurement methods. But even so, you can use certain rule-of-thumb devices to get a better idea than you may now have about the results of our advertising.

WHAT RESULTS DO YOU EXPECT?

Essentially, measuring results means comparing sales with advertising. In order to do it you have to start early in the process—before you even make up the advertisement. The question to answer is: What do you expect the advertising to do for your store?

In thinking about the kinds of results to expect, it is helpful to divide advertising into two basic kinds, immediate-response advertising and attitude advertising.

IMMEDIATE-RESPONSE ADVERTISING

This type of advertising is designed to cause the potential customer to buy a particular product from you within a short time—today, tomorrow, the weekend, or next week. An example of such decision-triggering ads is one that promotes regular price merchandise with immediate appeal. Other examples are ads which use

160

price appeals in combination with clearance sales, special purchases, seasonal items (for example, white sales, Easter sales, etc.), and "family-of-items" purchases.

Such advertising should be checked for results daily or at the end of one week from appearance. Because all advertising has some carry-over effect, it is a good idea to check also at the end of two weeks from appearances, three weeks from appearances, and so on, to ensure that no opportunity for using profit-making messages is lost.

ATTITUDE ADVERTISING

This type of advertising is used to keep your store's name and merchandise before the public. Some people think of this type as "image-building" advertising. With it, you remind people week after week about your regular merchandise or services or tell them about new or special services or policies. Such advertising should create in the minds of your customers the attitude you want them to have about your store, its merchandise, its services, and its policies. It is your reputation-builder. To some degree, all advertising should be attitude advertising.

Attitude (or image-building) advertising is harder to measure than immediate-response advertising because you cannot always attribute a specific sale to it. Its sales are usually created long after the ad has appeared and are triggered by the customer some time after having seen the ad. However, you should keep in mind that there is a lead time relationship in such advertising. For example, an ad or a series of ads that announces you have the exclusive franchise for a particular brand probably starts to pay off when you begin to get customers who want that brand only and ask no questions about competing brands.

In short, attitude-advertising messages linger in the minds of those who have some contact with the ad. Sooner or later, these messages are used by people when they decide that they will make a particular purchase.

Because the purpose of attitude advertising is spread out over an extended period of time, the measurement of results can be more leisurely. Some attitude advertising—such as a series of ads about the brands which the store carries—can be measured at the end of one month from the appearance of the ads or at the end of a campaign.

PLANNING FOR RESULTS

Whether you are trying to measure immediate response or attitude advertising, your success will depend on how well the ads have been planned. The trick is to work out points against which you can check after customers have seen or heard the advertising.

Certain things are basic to planning advertisements whose results can be measured. First of all, *advertise products or services that have merit in themselves.* Unless a product or service is good, few customers will make repeat purchases no matter how much advertising the store does.

Many people will not make an initial purchase of a shoddy item because of doubt or unfavorable word-of-mouth publicity. The ad that successfully sells inferior merchandise usually loses customers in the long run.

Small marketers, as a rule, should *treat their messages seriously.* Humor is risky as well as difficult to write. Be on the safe side and tell people the facts about your merchandise and services.

Another basic element in planning advertisements is to *know exactly what you wish a particular ad to accomplish.* In an immediate-response ad, you want customers to come in and buy a certain item or items in the next several days. In attitude advertising, you decide what attitude you are trying to create and plan each individual ad to that end. In a small operation, the ads usually feature merchandise rather than store policies.

Plan the ad around only one idea. Each ad should have a single message. If the message needs reinforcing with other ideas, keep them in the background. If you have several important things to say, use a different ad for each one and run the ads on succeeding days or weeks.

The pointers which follow are intended to help you plan ads that will make your store stand out when people read or hear about it.

> ► *Identify your store fully and clearly.* Logotypes or signatures in printed ads should be clear, uncluttered, and prominently displayed. Give your address and telephone number. Radio and television announcements to identify your sponsorship should be full and as frequent as possible without interfering with the message.
>
> ► *Pick illustrations that are similar in character.* Graphics—that is, drawings, photos, borders, and layout—that are similar in character help people to recognize your advertising immediately.

▶ *Select a printing typeface and stick to it.* Using the same typeface or the same audio format on radio or television helps people to recognize your ads. Also using the same sort of type and illustrations in all ads allows you to concentrate on the message when examining changes in response to ads.

▶ *Make copy easy to read.* The printed message should be broken up with white space to permit the reader to see the lines quickly.

▶ *Use coupons for direct-mail advertising response as often as possible.* Coupons give an immediate sales check. Key the coupon in some manner so that you can measure the response easily.

▶ *Get the audience's attention in the first five seconds of the radio and TV commercial.* Also, state your main message in the first sentence if possible.

TESTS FOR IMMEDIATE-RESPONSE ADS

In weighing the results of your *immediate*-response advertisements the following devices should be helpful:

COUPONS RETURNED

Usually these coupons represent sales of the product. When the coupons represent requests for additional information or contact with a salesperson, were enough leads obtained to pay for the ad? If the coupon is dated, you can determine the number of returns for the first, second, and third weeks.

REQUESTS BY PHONE OR LETTER REFERRING TO THE AD

A "hidden offer" can cause people to call or write. Include—for example, in the middle of a paragraph—a statement that on request the product or additional information will be supplied. Results should be checked weekly over a six- or twelve-month period because this type of ad may have considerable carry-over effect.

163

SPLIT
RUNS BY
NEWSPAPERS

Prepare two ads (different in some way you would like to test) and run them on the same day. Identify the ads—in the message or with a coded coupon—so you can tell them apart. Ask customers to bring in the ad or coupon. When you place the ad, ask the newspaper to give you a split run—that is: to print "ad A" in part of its press run and "ad B" in the rest of the run. Count the responses to each ad.

SALES
MADE OF
PARTICULAR
ITEM

If the ad is for a bargain or limited-time offer, you can consider that sales at the end of one week, two weeks, three weeks, and four weeks came from the ad. You may need to make a judgment to estimate how many sales resulted from display and personal selling.

CHECK
STORE
TRAFFIC

An important function of advertising is to build store traffic which results in purchases of items that are not advertised. Pilot studies show, for example, that many customers who are brought to the store by an ad for a blouse also bought a handbag. Some bought the bag in addition to the blouse, others instead of the blouse.

You may be able to use a local college or high school distributive-education class to check store traffic. Class members could interview customers as they leave the store to determine: (1) which advertised items they bought, (2) what other items they bought, and (3) what they shopped for but did not buy.

TESTING ATTITUDE
ADVERTISING

When advertising is spread out over one selling season or several seasons, part of the measurement job is keeping records. Your aim is to compare records of ads and sales for an extended time.

An easy way to set up a file is by marking the date of appearance on tear sheets of newspaper ads, log reports of radio and television ads, and copies of direct-mail ads. The file may be broken down into monthly, quarterly, or semiannual blocks. By recording the sales of the advertised items on each ad or log, you can make comparisons.

In *attitude (or image-building) advertising,* the individual ads are building blocks, so to speak, which make up your advertising program over a selling season. The problem is trying to measure each ad and the effects of all of the ads taken together.

164

One approach is to make your comparisons on a weekly basis. If you run an ad each week, at the end of the first week after the ad appears, compare that week's sales with sales for the same week a year ago. At the end of the second week, compare your sales with those of the end of the first week as well as with those of a year ago.

At the end of the *third* week, and then one month, three months, six months, and twelve months after the appearance of the ad, repeat the process even though additional ads may have appeared in the meantime. For each of these ads, you should also make the same type of comparisons. You will, of course, be measuring the "momentum" of all of your ads as well as the results of a single ad. You might find it useful to place your figures on a form such as that shown in Table 13.1.

After a time, you probably will be able to estimate how much is due to the individual ad and how much to the momentum of all of your advertising. You may then make changes in specific details of the ad to increase response.

When comparing sales increases over some preceding period, allowances must be made for situations that are not normal. For example, your experience may be that rain on the day an ad appears cuts its pulling power by 50 percent. Similarly, advertising response will be affected by the fact that your customers work in a factory that is out on strike.

Some of the techniques which you can use for keeping on top of and improving attitude advertising follow.

REPEAT

REPEAT AN AD

If response to an ad is good, run it—without change—two or three times and check the responses to each appearance against previous appearances.

Keep repeating the process. Much advertising loses effectiveness because the advertiser doesn't keep reminding people. Repetition helps increase knowledge of, and interest in, the product. You can soon estimate how often you should repeat each ad—exactly or with minor changes.

ANALYZE ALL ADS IN RELATION TO RESPONSE

Divide ads into at least two classes: high-response ads and low-response ads. Then look for differences between the two classes.

TABLE 13.1
Ad-Results Monitoring

MEDIA	PRODUCT	SALES WEEK 1	SALES WEEK 2	SALES WEEK 3	TOTAL MONTHLY	REMARKS

DATES OF AD RUN From _____ to _____

ELEMENTS THAT MAY HAVE AFFECTED RESULTS:

DATE   ELEMENTS

OVERALL EVALUATION OF THE PERFORMANCE OF THIS AD.

The time the ad was run may be responsible for a particular response level. Other factors, however, may be just as influential—or more influential—than time. Consider the feature subject used in the illustration, persons shown, activities shown, types of merchandise, settings or backgrounds, and different colors used. Also consider the message and how well it was expressed. Did the copy stick to the theme? Or did it wander? If slogans were used, did they help make the point?

Graphic elements may be important. Check to see which response category is associated with the presence of coupons, borders, display lines, and small or incidental illustrations. Check response in relation to any variation in the way each appears. Compare any difference in type size and design or the boldness of the type.

Emphasis on brand names should also be checked. Price figures should be analyzed. If price lines are involved either in the ad or in the merchandise line of which the advertised product is a part, you should consider them also.

Check the size of the ad. It usually has a bearing on response. As a general rule, the larger the ad, the greater the response.

TRY TO
SEE A
PATTERN OF
DOMINANCE

Your analysis of high-and-low response ads may show that certain details—such as certain picture subjects—make the difference between a high or low response. Try to find the combinations that work best for your firm and merchandise.

NOTE
CHANGES
OCCURRING
OVER TIME

A small retailer should never take a winning combination for granted. There is no single formula that will ensure high-response ads every time. Advertising changes. Therefore, you should watch the ads of others to see what changes are occurring. Continue to analyze your own ads, make small changes occasionally, and note any variations in response.

LISTEN
TO WHAT
PEOPLE SAY
ABOUT
YOUR ADS

As you listen, try to discover the mental framework within which any comment about your ad was made. Then try to find points that reinforce believability and a feeling that your product fulfills some wish or need.

Be careful that you are not misled by what people say. An ad can cause a great deal of comment yet bring in practically no sales. An ad may be so beautiful or clever that as far as the customer is concerned the sales message is lost.

WHEN YOU USE SEVERAL MEDIA

When your ads appear simultaneously in different media—such as the newspaper, on radio and television, in direct-mail pieces, and as handbills—you should try to evaluate the relative effectiveness of each one. You can check one printed medium against the other by using companion (the same or almost identical) ads in the newspaper, direct mail, and handbills.

You can make the job of analyzing and comparing results from the various media easier by varying your copy—the message. Your ad copy thus becomes the means of identifying your ad response.

You can check broadcast media—radio and TV—by slanting your message. Suppose, for example, that you advertise an item at a 20-percent reduction. Your radio or TV ad might say something like this: "Come in and tell us you want this product at 20-percent off."

You can compare these responses with results from your "20-percent-off" newspaper ad. Require the customer to bring in the newspaper ad—or a coupon from it.

Some of the ways to vary the copy include combining the brand name with one word or a few words indicating the product type, picture variations, size variations, and color variations. You might use the last three to check your printed ads against each other as well as against your radio and TV ads.

Be careful that the copy variation is not so great that a different impression is received from each medium. Here you would, in effect, have two different ads.

14
PUBLIC RELATIONS

THE CONFLICT OF IMAGE PERCEPTION

A conflict of image perception is the basic small-business public-relations problem today. Your own business has changed, but the image in the mind of the public either hasn't changed or never existed with any degree of clarity.

Most people associate public relations with publicity and this causes them to believe that the effectiveness of a program can be judged by the number of column inches published in the newspapers or by the minutes of air time secured through radio and TV. This notion is false.

CHANGE OF PUBLIC ATTITUDES

An effective public-relations program is one that creates a positive change in attitude within a defined target public. Only when that positive change of attitude has occurred—and within the desired public—has your program been a success. Only then will your self-image and your public image converge as reality.

The mass of human beings, taken collectively, is normally referred to as "the public." Assuming that you want to effect a change in the public image of your business, it should be obvious that you can't reach all America's millions by placing a news release in your local newspaper, whatever its circulation. Not everyone takes a newspaper. Not everyone who takes one reads it. Not everyone who reads it reads all of it. And not everyone who reads a part of it cares one way or the other about much of what he or she reads. The same is true for other media. No single communications medium can reach the mass public. Effective public relations deals with more limited publics, publics which are characterized by certain similarities.

DEFINE TARGET PUBLICS In public relations a public is defined as any group of individuals which the program seeks to influence. True, it may be a mass public. But more frequently it is a limited one. Different publics are influenced in different ways. Ethnic minorities are reached differently than are corporate executives. The difference is more than a difference of medium. It involves special themes and styles of delivery.

Once the desired public or publics is identified, the question becomes "how are they reached?" Media selection is a crucial aspect of effective public relations. Most apparent are the mass media—regional newspapers, wire services, network broadcasting, and telecasting.

SUIT THE MEDIA TO THE PUBLIC Mass coverage may completely miss a special target or may discredit the message. A limited medium which has credibility with the target public may be a much better approach—especially if a change of attitude rather than column inches is sought. A country weekly may be better than a major daily; a local radio station, more suitable than regional TV; a professional journal better than a national news magazine.

The message also must be tailored to the public. What message is it that you wish your public to hear? What will best characterize the image of your organization? What response do you wish to evoke from a given public by the message you offer? In public relations, this message is called a "theme."

THEMES CONVEY IMAGES Certain themes reflect the image conveyed to the various publics. Choose these themes cautiously. Make sure they honestly reflect the business's current objectives and accomplishments. Be certain they tell a true story: honesty and integrity are basic to good public relations. Once themes have been selected, decide which ones to emphasize with each important public.

MATCH THEMES TO PUBLICS Communicate to a given public the themes that are most likely to evoke the desired response from that public. From potential members, the desired response is membership; from potential sponsors, it is money; from government leaders, it is favorable legislation; and from the *general public,* it is goodwill.

In dealing with publics and the media, there is one consideration which is so basic that it is frequently overlooked, yet it must be con-

170

sciously and deliberately cultivated in an effective public-relations program. It is, simply, this: for *every* public and *every* medium there are a few key individuals who serve as opinion makers. The attitudes of these few individuals are crucial in determining the attitudes of a public over which they have influence.

INFLUENTIALS: KEY TO PUBLICS

These decision makers and opinion makers are the *influentials*. They are important enough to the public-relations effort to warrant special attention, including frequent personal contact. Developing and maintaining contact with influentials is essential. For instance, whether or not a story is printed or included in a newscast may depend more on your relationship with the News Editor or News Director than on the merits of the story. The success of an important project in the community may depend entirely on the attitudes of the leadership in that community toward your business. The job of effecting a change of attitude within a given public can be made much easier if you can develop a positive relationship with the influentials of that public.

What is a public-relations program? It is a sequence of planned activities designed to communicate a positive image of your organization to its important publics. Essentially, what is being communicated is the basic objectives of the organization, normally expressed through projects or events. The first step, then, is to define clearly themes which are to be directed to target publics, the primary objectives of the business or organization.

Why does your business exist? What objectives justify the projects you conduct? One reason for a confused public image is that the organization lacks clearly established goals and objectives—in other words, it has no uniform themes to communicate. Every organization should have clearly stated goals and objectives in written form. Every project should proceed from a stated objective consistent with the general objectives of the organization or business. These two simple guidelines are essential to an effective public-relations program. *Every planned business or event is a public-relations opportunity.*

ALL PROGRAMS— PUBLIC RELATIONS EVENTS

The program itself is a public-relations event. Public relations should be either the primary or the secondary objective of every planned activity. As such, it should be programmed with the activity.

ONE PERSON
IN CHARGE

Every public-relations program should have a single co-ordinator who is responsible for planning and implementing all public-relations activities. He or she may direct the work of assistants who are more routinely involved in projects. It is his or her task to ensure that the entire program is well coordinated and effectively administered. This individual is the principal contact with the media and should control all releases.

Your business or organization may not exist in the mind of the public in the same way it exists in your own mind. There may be a conflict of image perception. But if you will consider public relations as more than publicity; if you will take time to identify your publics, establish your themes, and choose your media; if you will do it consistently with every project; if you will establish contact with key influentials and cultivate a positive relationship; and if your public-relations director has the authority to coordinate the program, then the conflict will gradually become less and less pronounced. Your business will become more and more effective, and you will begin to know the meaning and the importance of good public relations.

BASIC STEPS
TO SOLID PUBLIC
RELATIONS

START
WITH A
PLAN OF
ACTION

Before you can begin your public-relations plan of action, you need considerable input. You should start the year by delineating overall objectives of the organiztion with plans of action for how to get there. Once this is done, you can finalize your programs and projects knowing that the objectives of each support the overall organizational objectives.

SELECT
YOUR
THEME

Once you have selected your target publics, select the theme of your story to appeal to the particular interests of these publics. Often your media contacts will cooperate in pinpointing features aimed at your publics as well as assist in preparing your news stories for them.

At this point you can prepare your plan of action for the year in as much detail as you feel is necessary. For example, you might list every news release and news conference for every project in chronological order detailing the target publics and theme of each many months in advance. With preplanning such as this it is relatively simple to follow the master plan, using it primarily as a checklist.

INFLUENTIALS

The influentials most essential to the success of your program are the decision makers at your media: your newspaper editors, your radio and television news directors, and the like.

When and how you make your initial contact with your local media influentials is vital to the success of your relationship with them. Pay them the courtesy of an introductory call *before* you need their help on a specific project. Start with a list of the news directors at your television and radio stations and the city editors at your newspapers. Depending on the size of the staff at each medium, you may need to expand your list to include newscasters and editors of special-interest newspaper selections. Call each media contact to make an advance appointment at a time convenient for him or her. Be well prepared to discuss the objectives and projects of your business or organization and answer questions concerning them. Be prompt, brief, and businesslike. Keep in mind that media people are very busy. Explain who you are, why you're there, and what newsworthy events are planned for the coming months. Have either a business card or a sheet of paper listing your name, mailing address, and phone number to leave with your contacts. Ask the newspaper what its deadlines are and what it needs from you. People who work at the newspaper can tell you how best to submit your copy. They may also ask you to remind them of upcoming events or to be put on the mailing list for advance information.

Once the organization's objectives are in hand, begin your PR plan. First, each program and project should be carefully checked to make certain the objectives of each support and coordinate with the overall objectives of your organization. If they are obviously at cross purposes, you should strongly consider dropping the out-of-step program or project. Now you have some clear-cut objectives with all of your programs and projects supporting these and the plans of action on each.

At this point, you should take a hard, objective look at each to see which are newsworthy. This isn't easy. Of course, everything you're doing is interesting to you and to your business, but that's not the point. You must learn to recognize and use for publicity only those things that will interest others. Do not expect your community's editor or news director to tell readers something about which they couldn't care less.

His or her job depends on the ability to gather news that will capture the general public's interest. To establish the necessary rapport with your local media, you must establish yourself as a source of good, hard news.

If you discover that your organization or business isn't doing much that is of interest to outsiders, it is your responsibility to originate some projects which are newsworthy. This is critical. How can you hope to get your name in the news if you're not doing anything of interest?

SELECT YOUR PUBLICS

Selectivity makes the difference between success and failure in meeting your objectives. The difference between amateurish and professional public-relations programs is that amateurs think first of the story while professionals think first of their target audience and then tailor the story to that audience. First decide what audience you want to reach. Then select media to reach audiences where you're weakest. This may mean sectional newspapers, ethnic publications, or corporate house organs. Decide what groups of people are your most logical prospects, then select your media to reach them.

Keep in mind that all media have special-interest features catering to different audiences. By selecting these carefully, you can reach target publics in virtually any age group, socioeconomic level, ethnic group, income level, or whatever other criterion you might desire.

Media influentials in large cities may not have time to grant you a personal visit. If this is the case, handle your first call on the telephone. In any case, follow up on the first contact with a letter of thanks for the courtesy. Confirm any instructions you may have received and indicate that you are looking forward to working together.

WRITING YOUR RELEASE

Different media prefer to have stories submitted in different ways. This section will be limited to fact outlines and news releases. These can be submitted to all media.

Fact outlines should be typed double or triple spaced on 8½" x 11" white paper. From a fact outline, your media contact must be able to get enough information to write a finished story.

In news releases the who, what, when, where, why, and, if possible, the how should be included in the first two or three paragraphs. Good stories are written in "inverted-pyramid style." That means that the most important information appears first, and other items appear in

174

order of descending importance down to miscellaneous background information. The reason for this is that media people like to be able to cut the bottom of a story to make it fit an available time or space slot. Each paragraph should be written so that, if every one below it were deleted, the remaining story would still tell the essential facts.

1. Never use the word "publicity" when talking to the media. Your media contacts are interested only in news, not in whether you get any publicity.

2. Honor the life of a news story. The life of a story is the period in which it is news. In order to be news, it must be timely. The longer you wait to hand in your story, the weaker it becomes.

3. Don't talk "inside" business information to the media. Be sure to explain what you're talking about. Don't leave the media guessing.

4. Include complete, accurate details. Be factual, not fancy. If your media contacts must call you back or call somebody else to complete your story, you might not be doing your job.

5. Honor the almighty deadline: don't bother your contacts when you know they're close to a deadline. Always submit your news to comply with their deadlines.

6. Don't insult a photographer. Television and newspaper photographers are professionals. Be on hand to introduce them and give them accurate identification of their subjects, but let them choose their subjects and stage their own shots.

7. Don't be a nuisance. Don't repeatedly call your contacts to see when your story will be used. Never phone your contacts at their homes unless you're certain you have urgent news. Even then, it's best to wait until you can talk with them during their business hours, if possible.

8. Follow through. You can give your contacts the best possible advance news coverage, but if you don't make certain they get all of the on-the-spot help they need at the event, you haven't done your job.

175

FORMAT
FOR NEWS
RELEASES

1. Use white 8½" x 11" paper of good quality.

2. You are the contact for the media in case they need more information, so write your name, address, and phone number in the upper left- or right-hand corner. This is called source information.

3. The release instructions go above the text. This is simply the date, possibly also the time of day, you want this information released. For example:

FOR IMMEDIATE RELEASE

or

FOR EVENING EDITION

Monday, January 5

or

FOR RELEASE

Wednesday, March 9

4. Type only on the front side of the paper using double or triple spacing.

5. If your release is more than one page long, each page should be numbered and the word "more" should be at the bottom of each page except the last. The story should be closed by -30- or "###."

6. End each page at the end of a paragraph.

7. Use simple, short-to-medium sentences and avoid editorial comment, personal opinions, excessive adjectives, and conclusions.

8. Be brief. Try to keep your releases to one page or a maximum of two pages. Two pages double spaced will about fill 12 column inches, which is more space than you will normally be given.

9. Always use exact dates and times in your releases rather than "tomorrow" or "next month."

10. List the addresses as well as the name of event location(s).

11. Never begin a sentence with numbers. Spell out numbers from one to ten, then use numerals from 11 on up.

GLOSSARY OF ADVERTISING TERMS

Account A client whose advertising is prepared and executed by an advertising agency.

Account Executive The advertising agency's representative whose responsibility is the coordination of planning and the execution of client advertising programs.

Advertiser A company or individual using a variety of media to communicate with selected audiences in an attempt to promote the advertiser's products and/or services.

Advertising Communication of a message through a paid medium (e.g., magazines) with the intent to influence people to purchase a product or service or otherwise act.

Advertising Agency A firm that plans, prepares, and executes advertising programs for clients, including preparing art and copy, selecting and placing media, and conducting research..

Advertising Budget The allocation of funds to promote a company's products or services (e.g., funds spent on media and ad preparation).

Advertising Manager A company executive responsible for developing advertising programs in coordination with the advertising agency.

Advertising Department A company department which acts as liaison with the advertising agency or otherwise conducts advertising programs in-house.

Advertising Effectiveness Determination whether advertising has accomplished its objectives (e.g., increased inquiries, sales, favorable attitudes, awareness).

178

Advertising Plan	The advertising program, budget, and reasons underlying media selection.
Agate Line	A newspaper measurement, one column wide and one-fourteenth of an inch deep.
Agency Commission	A discount, usually 15 percent, which is allowed to qualified advertising agencies by media for the agencies' purchase of space or time.
Aided-Recall	A technique to determine if readers remember seeing certain advertisements. The interviewer gives the respondent a clue to refocus attention on the original exposure situation, then asks the respondent to name the company or product advertised.
Airbrush	A pressure gun shaped like a pencil that sprays ink by means of compressed air. Used to obtain tone or graduated effects in artwork and to "correct" imperfect black-and-white photos.
Art Director	The person preparing or supervising preparation of graphic elements of advertisements and catalogs, including layouts, photography, illustrations, finished artwork, and printing.
Associated Business Press	An organization of trade media.
Association of Industrial Advertisers (AIA)	A national organization for the overall improvement of standards and practices used in industrial advertising.
Attitude	The feeling or emotional element of experience. The "I like" or "I dislike" aroused by something or someone. The goal is to shift these attitudes toward a favorable reaction toward your company or products.
Audience	The persons to whom your advertising message is directed.
Audit Bureau of Circulations (ABC)	Sponsors advertisers, agencies, and publishers for accurate and informative circulation statistics.
Average Net Paid Circulation	A figure that indicates the average number of copies of a publication sold for an issue for a specific time period, excluding complimentary copies.
Backing up	Printing both sides of a sheet of paper.
Ben Day	An engraving process permitting the production of halftone or color effects without halftone screens.
Billing	Money expended by an advertising agency for its clients in the purchase of space, time, and other services.
Bleed	To extend type or illustration to the edge of a page.

179

Blowup An enlargement.

Body Type Type used for the main body or text of an advertisement.

Boldface Heavy dark typeface used for emphasis in headings, subheadings, etc.

Brochure A pamphlet (on a specific product or service) bound in the form of a booklet.

Business Publication Audit (BPA) An independent firm which audits the circulation of business publications to determine how many people of each classification are receiving the publication.

Business Publications Magazines with editorial matter directed to particular industries, businesses, or professions.

Camera Copy Material ready to be photographed for platemaking.

Campaign All advertising and related efforts on behalf of a product or service, directed toward the attainment of predetermined objectives.

Catalogs A systematic listing of a company's products or services with detailed descriptions of specifications, applications, and benefits; and sometimes including pricing and shipping information.

Center Spread An advertisement appearing on two facing pages printed as a single sheet in the center of a publication.

Checking Verifying that an advertisement appeared in media as ordered.

Checking Copy The copy of a publication sent to an advertiser or agency to prove that an advertisement appeared as ordered.

Circulation The total universe or segments of audience to which a publication is directed or received.

Client A company whose advertising is prepared and executed by an advertising agency.

Clipping Bureaus Firms specializing in clipping advertisements and news items concerning individuals, companies, products, etc. Such clips help evaluate effectiveness of promotional campaign. Charges vary depending on quantity of clips.

Closing Date The date or hour set as a deadline for submitting insertion orders plus copy material for printing in specific publications.

Coated Paper Paper which has a surface coating, giving it a smooth, often glossy finish.

Collating Putting sheets in proper sequence before binding.

180

Collateral All material prepared by the agency which does not earn a media commission, (e.g., point-of-purchase, direct mail, catalogs, and packing).

Combination Plate In photoengraving, halftone and line work combined on one plate; etched for both halftone and line depth.

Comprehensive ("Comp") A layout simulating the actual appearance of an advertisement, usually with real or simulated type and photostat of illustrations pasted in place.

Continuous Tone A photographic image which has not been screened and which contains gradient tones from black to white.

Controlled Circulation Publication circulation in which the audience is carefully screened as to job function, title, company, industry, and so forth, to assure readership of a specified type for advertisers.

Contrast Total comparison of highlights and shadows in an original or reproduction.

Cooperative Advertising Manufacturers allocate certain portions of their total advertising budgets for use by local distributors and dealers (and cost is shared by both parties).

Copy Written material used in advertisements or brochures, as opposed to the illustration and layout.

Copy Theme The main appeal of the product or service as presented by the printed word in the form of an advertisement.

Copywriter One who writes the text for ads, commercials, catalogs, brochures, publicity releases, or other advertising-related media.

Cost per Thousand (CPM) A dollar figure used to evaluate the relative cost of various media.

Creative Strategy An outline of the basic decisions (e.g., whom to sell, how to sell, what to sell, and the way of selling) necessary to organize the ideas which then will be translated into the advertisements of the campaign.

Crop To cut down in size, usually a photo or plate.

Demographics Statistics and characteristics of a specified population

Direct-Mail Advertising Mailing promotional materials (e.g., printed letters, booklets, circulars, and catalogs) to specialized or general prospective users.

Directories Publications listing membership in an organization or industry, or otherwise listing products and services supplied by different manufacturers in specific industries or territories.

Display Type Type set larger than the text; used to attract attention.

Double Spread	Two facing pages in a publication used for a single, unbroken advertisement (also center spread).
Dummy	A paste-up or pattern of a proposed printed piece.
Embossing	Letters or artwork impressed in relief to get a raised surface; can be done on a blank paper or over other printing.
Engraving	Any printing plate produced by an etching or cutting process.
Execution	The translation into words, pictures, or motion, of the ideas presented in the creative strategy.
Flush Left (or Right)	Type matter set to line up at the left or right margin.
Font	An assortment of letters and characters in one size and style.
Format	Size, style, shape, and printing requirements of any magazine, catalog, or printed piece.
Four-Color Process	A printing process using a combination of four photoengravings, each with a different color ink, to reproduce color artwork which has been reduced to basic colors by a filtration process.
Fractional Space	Size of advertisement less than a full page.
Frequency	The number of times a particular medium or publication is used.
Galley Proofs	Proofs taken on sheets approximately 20 inches long, and impressed from type in galley trays before being separated into pages. It is a proof of what you'll actually get in type.
Gravure	A printing process permitting a number of impressions to be made in a single operation at high speed.
Halftone	Tone gradation achieved by a large number of dots of varying size made by exposing a negative through a halftone screen.
Horizontal Publication	A publication intended to reach a broad audience across many industries (as opposed to vertical publications within a single industry).
House Agency	An advertising agency controlled in whole or in part by one advertiser.
House Organ	A company publication devoted to its own interests.
Impression	The pressure of type or plate as it comes in contact with the paper when being printed.

Inquiry Test A check of the effectiveness of advertisements on the basis of number of inquiries returned per advertisement.

Inserts (1) Enclosures to other letters or packages; (2) messages printed by the advertiser to be inserted and bound in a specific publication. Inserts can be on special stock or in color different from publications.

Insertion Order Advertiser- or agency-written instructions to a publisher requesting space for insertion of a specific advertisement size, on a given date, at an agreed rate, with other instructions as to color, bleeds, etc.

Justify To space out lines so they are all exactly the same length.

Layout A drawing or sketch of the proposed printed piece or advertisement.

Letterpress Printing Printing by pressing an inked raised surface to the printing surface.

Logotype (Logo) A specially created design or symbol used to identify a company or product.

Mechanical A composite of the elements of an advertisement to show their relative size and placement.

Media (1) Broad tools used to communicate with specific audiences (e.g., advertising, public relations, trade shows); (2) the specific advertising vehicles, including newspapers, trade publications, films, radio, television, and billboards.

Motivation Research Attempts to uncover behavior or opinion motives.

Offset Printing The impression is transferred from the printing plate to a rubber blanket and then printed on paper.

One-Time Rate The cost of advertising one time. This rate is always higher since there is no frequency discount.

Opacity A property of paper which minimizes show through of printing from the reverse side or the next sheet.

Overrun Extra copies of printed material beyond the number ordered.

Pass-Along Readership Readers of a publication other than the original subscribers.

Paste-up Preparation of copy by putting all elements in proper position before the engraving process begins.

Percent-of-Sales Concept A budgeting term used to determine how much to spend for advertising as a percent of total sales.

GLOSSARY OF
ADVERTISING TERMS

Position	An advertisement's place on a page and the location of the page in the publication.
Preprint	A reproduction of an advertisement before it appears in a publication.
Pretesting	The testing of advertisements or parts of advertisements for effectiveness before they have appeared as part of a campaign.
Press Proof	A finished proof taken on the press in one or more colors, after proper make-ready.
Progressive Proofs	For color-process printing, the engraver or platemaker prepares a set of proofs showing each color separately and then in combination.
Pulling Power	The ability of an advertisement to attract favorable attention and produce returns in the form of inquiries and sales.
Ragged Left (or Right)	Successive lines in a body of type are set "staggered," or not flush to the left or right margin. Usually used for a special effect.
Rate Book	Compilations of rates charged by periodicals for use of a specified number of advertising pages.
Reader Recall	Testing whether the reader recalls seeing the advertisement in question.
Readership	The number of persons who read a publication, and the associated degree of attention given to each advertisement.
Recognition	A method of testing whether a specific audience recognizes a company's name, products, or campaign theme.
Retouching	The process of correcting or improving artwork and photographs before engravings are made.
Rough	A quick sketch of a concept so that a visual idea of the completed advertisement can be determined and reviewed before preparation of final art, copy, and production work.
Run	The total number of copies printed.
Space Representative	The publishers' agents or employees who sell advertising space in selected publications. Some representatives work for more than one publication or publisher at a time.
Score	To impress or indent a mark in paper with a string or rule to make folding easier.

Screen	Plate glass or film with cross-ruled opaque lines, used in cameras to break continuous-tone illustrations and art into halftones.
Standard Rate and Data Service	A service providing information on rates, deadlines, specifications, etc., for advertising in specific publications, newspapers, radio, and television.
Stock	Choice of paper, including thickness, color, and texture.
Tabloid	A newspaper or news magazine (usually relating to new products and literature) which is half the page size of the standard newspaper.
Tear Sheet	A page or section taken from a publication to prove that it actually ran, or to use in additional promotions.
Trade Publications	Publications having specialized circulations featuring articles, data, and advertisements on specific industries.
Vertical Media	Media directed at specific segments or industries (e.g., computers), as opposed to horizontal media.
Wasted Circulation	People in the audience of a magazine who are not prospects for a particular advertised product.
Web	Continuous roll of paper being fed into a printing press.
Work and Tumble	Printing the second side of a sheet by turning over from gripper to back, using same side guide.
Work and Turn	Printing the second side of a sheet by turning it over left to right, using the same edge of paper as a gripper.

TERMS USED
IN RADIO

AM Technically, amplitude modulation; practically, 550 to 1600 on the AM radio dial.

ARB American Research Bureau, a radio ratings organization that uses a diary method.

Adjacencies Commercials placed next to certain programming—news, weather, sports.

Affidavit A sworn statement that commercials were on air in certain time periods.

Affiliate A station, usually independently owned, that grants a network use of specific time periods for network programs and advertising. The remainder of the broadcast day is programmed locally.

Agency Commission Fifteen percent of your radio billing allowed to an accredited advertising agency, if it places your time.

Aided Recall One method of radio-audience survey where interviewer asks respondent: "Did you listen from 8 to 9 a.m.?"

Air-Check A tape made of a commercial or program at the time of airing.

All-News A station format that programs only news.

Announcement Commercial or spot. An ad of 60, 30, 20, or 10 seconds on radio.

Audience Survey A study of estimated listenings to various stations in a market. It usually shows the percentage of homes listening (homes using radio), the percent total listeners for each station (share of audience), or the total number of homes tuned to each station (ratings). While *homes* are surveyed in ARB

186

and Hooper, Pulse surveys *individuals*. Demographic information, cumulative audience, and out-of-home listening are also provided.

Availabilities Unsold time slots where commercials can be placed.

BTA Best times available—means same as run of station. It means that the station may schedule BTA or ROS announcements at times most advantageous to the station.

Broadcasting (1) Either of the electronic media: radio or television. (2) Sending out a signal on the airwaves capable of being received by a radio or television set.

Call Letters The station's name. Most stations east of the Mississippi River have call letters beginning with "W"; west of the Mississippi, call letters begin with "K" (with some exceptions both ways).

Campaign A planned radio-advertising drive.

Chain Break The time when a network affiliate identifies itself and delivers a commercial(s). The station may deliver commercials, too.

Coincidental Interview One method of surveying the radio audience where the individual is interviewed on the phone or in person about radio listening.

Combination Rate A reduced commercial rate available from stations with a geographical tie-in when *both* are bought.

Commercial See **announcement**.

Commercial Protection Specific time between competitive commercials and yours, granted by a station.

Contemporary Music Pop, also called Top-40.

Continuity Radio copy, scripts for commercials.

Contract Year A 12-month period during which commercial time is bought. The number of spots you buy in this time period entitles you to quantity discount.

Conversation Station Also called talk station. Refers to a station format that has lots of call-in and talking personality shows, little music.

Co-op Money contributed by a manufacturer or vendor to a store as partial payment for an ad.

Cost-per-Thousand The ratio of cost for radio time to each 1000 homes or listeners it reaches. If a station delivers 5000 homes for a $5.00 spot, the cpm is $1.00.

TERMS USED
IN RADIO

Country and Western A station format featuring country and western music.

Coverage Area The geographical area reached by a given station. It is based on a station's physical facilities and pattern of signal. A coverage map shows the areas covered. Most stations can provide you with such a map.

Cumulative Audience The audience reached by a station in two or more time periods or more than one station in a specified time period like a week. *Caution:* Be sure you know if a Cume figure is duplicated or unduplicated.

Day-Timer A radio station licensed by the FCC to operate in daytime only; i.e., sunup to sundown.

Dial Position The number at which the station is found on the radio dial. Also known as the station's frequency.

Diary One method of surveying the radio audience where the diary-keepers fill in the times they listen to radio.

Disc Jockey or Deejay A radio personality, usually on mostly-music stations. Besides playing the records, he or she provides service information, makes entertaining comments, and reads commercials.

Drivetime The morning and afternoon hours when listeners drive to and from work. Also called a.m. drivetime (6 to 10 a.m.) and p.m. drivetime (4 to 7 p.m.). Also called traffic time.

Duplication The quantity of multiple listenership in more than one spot. Example: Two spots on Tuesday on WXYZ may reach a total of 10,000 listeners (Impressions), but only 700 *different* (unduplicated) listeners.

End Rate The lowest rate at which a station offers commercial time.

ET Electrical transcription for playing on a turntable. The recorded message, usually a commercial. Also specifically the part of your commercial that's recorded, e.g., the musical logo as opposed to the live copy portion.

Ethnic Radio A station format directed toward one or more ethnic groups, e.g., Negro, Spanish, German, Polish, etc.

Evening Radio time usually from 7 p.m. to 10 p.m. or midnight, depending on station's sign-off time.

FCC Federal Communications Commission. The federal bureau that regulates number of stations, power, broadcast hours, etc. The FCC also compiles broadcast statistics.

188

Fixed Position A spot delivered at a guaranteed specific time, like 8:02 a.m.

Flight The period during which advertisers run their spots who are not 52-week advertisers. Fall flight, December flight, and the like.

Format The kind of programming a station does: middle-of-road, contemporary, all-news, talk, classical, country-western, etc.

Frequency The number of times a household or individual is in the radio audience in a week.

Frequency Discount A plan available from many stations for buying commercials at a lower rate when you run every week for 13, 26, 39, or 52 weeks or a minimum number of times *per week*. (Also called quality discount).

Full-Time Station A station that is allowed but not required by the FCC to be on the air 24 hours a day. Some full-time stations sign off at 10 p.m., some at midnight, and some never sign off.

General Rate See national rate.

Hiatus Time off the air. Usual application is when store budgets heavily in one month, takes a week's hiatus immediately afterwards.

Homes Using Radio (H.U.R.) Radios in use at a given time. A term used in audience measurement, expressed in percentage of total area homes, as well as total homes.

Hooper A rating service that surveys radio audience by coincidental telephone calls.

Housewife Time The hours usually between 10 a.m. and 4 p.m. in the broadcast day, when housewives are readily and economically reached by radio.

ID Short for identification. It usually refers to a 10-second commercial that does little more than keep a name before the public.

Image A kind of radio campaign conducted by many stores to change or polish the view customers have of it.

Independent A station not affiliated with a network.

In-Home Audience Radio listeners in the home.

Jingle A musical signature or logo frequently used by stores to identify themselves immediately on the air. Much like a store logo in a newspaper ad.

Kilocycle A number indicating a station's location on the radio dial and the physical characteristic of its broadcast signal: from 550 to 1600 kilocycles.

Live Copy Copy read by the station announcer in contrast to recorded tape commercials or ET's.

Live Tag A message added by an announcer to a recorded commercial to give local address, local price, etc. Often used when the manufacturer's radio commercials are aired by you locally.

Log Station record of times programs and commercials were on the air.

Logo A musical or sound signature used by the store to identify itself quickly.

Make-Good When your spot is not run, due to error or technical trouble, the station will run a spot at a later date; such a spot is a "make-good."

Megacycle The number of the station on the FM dial. From 88 to 108 megacycles.

Middle-of-Road A station format featuring mid-tempo music (show tunes, movie music, albums, etc.) with news, weather, and sports.

Minutes Commercials 60 seconds in length.

Monitor Recording of station's programming and commercials.

Morning Man Station personality hosting a.m. drivetime (6 to 10 a.m.) segment of broadcast day.

National Rate Rate offered to national (more than one market) advertisers on stations offering both local and national rates.

Network A group of stations affiliated with each other for common programming, at certain times of day—American Broadcasting System and National Broadcasting Company.

Nighttime The after-midnight hours of the radio broadcast day.

Open-End A recorded commercial that provides room at the end for a "tag."

Out-of-Home Audience Radio listeners to auto and transistor radios outside of home.

Package Plan Some combination of spots devised by a station and offered to advertisers at a special price. Package plans are usually weekly or monthly buys.

Participating Program A program shared by *several* advertisers rather than a sponsored program for one advertiser *alone*.

Permanent Sign-On The permanent time assigned by the FCC for some day-timers to go on the air (instead of sunrise).

190

Personality	A radio announcer who projects enthusiasm, believability, and reliability to the radio audience, persuading them to listen to the radio show and buy the products and services advertised.
Pick-Up	The point at which a program is picked up for airing. Could be a remote from a store, a sports show from a stadium, or a special event from another station.
Pop	Contemporary music.
Power	The amount of electricity (in watts) that a station operates on.
Preempt	To replace a regular program or commercial with something of greater interest, often political or sports broadcasts.
Premium Rate	An extra charge for especially valuable time—fixed position, news, special events, etc.
Program	A feature of any length, sponsored or unsponsored, aired by a station.
Pulse	A radio rating service that surveys audience by personal, in-home interviews and aided recall. It uses homes as the base.
Rate Holder	A spot run to preserve conditions of contract, for instance, being on every week of the year, if only with one :10 per week.
Rates	A station's charges for commercial time.
Rating Service	A company that surveys the radio audience for total homes or individuals listening, percentages of total listening for specific stations.
Reach	How many different households or individuals a given station, program, or commercial reaches in a given time period. Reach may also be measured for a series of commercials or campaigns.
Rebate	An extra discount on radio time when the advertiser uses more commercials than called for in the contract and earns a better rate.
Remote	A broadcast from some place other than station's own studio. Remotes are often done from stores for special events.
Renewal	The extension of existing contract on or before its expiration date.
Representative or Rep	A function designed to aid local stations in getting national business. When radio is bought regionally for more than one Sears store, a radio rep can be helpful in giving you facts, coverage, rates, etc., on a local station.

**TERMS USED
IN RADIO**

Retail Rate — Same as local rate (or lower).

Rhythm and Blues — A station format featuring contemporary music with high concentration of records by black performers.

Rights — Charges to a station for the right to broadcast a sporting event. If an event is sponsored, the sponsor usually pays the bill.

Rock 'n' Roll — A station format featuring popular music. Sometimes called contemporary sound or Top-40.

Run of Station (ROS) — Same as Best Time Available.

Sandwich — A kind of commercial where live copy runs in between musical open and close.

Saturation — Using a heavy schedule of commercials to get the message across to as many listeners as possible. A popular use of saturation is to advertise sale events.

Schedule — The times of day and dates an advertiser's commercials run in a specific campaign.

Scripts — Radio copy, also called continuity.

Separation — Commercial protection. The station provides a set time period between competitors.

Sets in Use — Radios turned on at any given time.

Share of Audience — The percent of tuned-in audience using each station at any given time.

Short Rate — A charge back to the advertiser for not fulfilling a contract.

Sign-Off — The time a station goes off the air. This is compulsory for day-timers and station's own decision for full-timers.

Sign-On — The time a station goes on air. Sun-up for daytimers or time assigned by FCC. Self-determined by full-timers.

Single-Rate Card — Station card where one time rate applies to both national and local advertisers.

Sixties — 60-second or minute commercials.

Sponsor — May be the advertiser who sponsors a radio program or may refer to any advertiser on a station.

Spot — A commercial or announcement.

192

Spot Radio (Also national spot) A national radio buy which allows an advertiser to buy commercials in many markets by buying individual stations, not necessarily affiliated with a network.

Strip A program or spot purchased at the same time each day.

Tag An announcement at end of a recorded commercial with added information; also music at end of live copy to set commercial off from other commercials.

Talent Radio performer.

Talk A station format consisting of telephone interviews, conversation with celebrities, informational shows, etc.

Tape To record a commercial (or other sound) for future on-air use. ˙

T.F. Til forbid. An advertising schedule without a fixed expiration date. It runs until the advertiser terminates.

Time Classification Various time segments during the broadcast day priced differently and denoted by Class AA, Class A, Class B, Class C, etc.

Total Audience Plan A spot package consisting of a combination of spots in each time classification that will reach all of the station's listeners in a specified time span.

Traffic Departments in ad agencies and stations which ensure that your commercials will get on the air.

Vertical Saturation Slotting commercials heavily on several stations one or two days before a sale and on the sale day itself, to reach the largest number of listeners.

THE RETAILER'S LANGUAGE

Action Item Merchandise that comes in and goes out fast, is reordered. Action items usually live a fast, but profitable, life. Also called winners, runners, items.

Ad Requisition Information sheets filled out by buyers to tell the advertising department all the facts about advertised merchandise. Requisitions ask pertinent questions that jog the buyer's memory. Copywriters write copy by reading requisitions and looking at actual merchandise.

Advertising Manager Many stores now have two: one for creative administration; the other for business matters. The manager may be head of sales promotion or advertising staff or may report to sales-promotion director. In some stores, the "advertising manager" supervises the print ads while broadcast ad manager is in charge of radio and TV.

Anniversary Sale Like the queen's "official birthday," an "anniversary sale" is not usually the store's real birthday but a convenient time to celebrate with a sale. Many stores have anniversary sales in October.

Art Also called artwork. The illustrations for print.

Assistant Buyer The buyer's runner. This job can be the first step on the road to promotion for an executive trainee or a dead end depending largely on the assistant's aptitude and aggressiveness and the buyer's generosity.

Bait and Switch A shady practice where a low-end item is advertised at an attractive price and the customer is talked into buying a higher priced item when he or she comes into the shop.

194

Bank Money a salesperson is issued daily by the accounting department in order to make change. A department's banker picks up the "banks" in the morning for sales personnel and deposits them at the end of the day.

BBB Better Business Bureau. Polices retail advertising and policies, guards against extravagant claims and misleading copy.

Beat Last Year Every buyer's ambition because if it is done consistently, it means a big bonus in January. It means bettering last year's sales figures on the corresponding day this year. The day is determined by a complicated retail calendar which includes such information as whether it rained or snowed or the merchandise didn't come in on last year's day-to-be-beaten.

Borax A highly promotional sale ad. Also called hard sell.

Boutique A small shop devoted to the latest fashions and accessories for younger men or women. Also such a shop within a large store.

Branches Suburban stores (often in shopping centers) that downtown stores started building after World War II to get suburban business and stem the inroads of discounters. Ordinarily branch operations are merchandised by main-store buyers with on-the-scene department managers who report to the branch-store manager—usually the most important executive in a branch.

Branch-Store Coordinators Usually between the assistant buyer and buyer in a store. "Coordinators" act as divisional merchandise managers in individual branches, are also responsible for branch ads in suburban newspapers, picking up sections of downtown ads. Coordinators usually outrank branch department managers; buyers outrank coordinators.

Budget Outline of store's (division or department) plan of spending for merchandise, operation expenses, and sales promotion to achieve a reasonable profit.

Bugs Little pictures in ads that illustrate something a buyer insists on. Prime example: a picture of sofa and chair styles available in ready-made slipcovers.

Build-Up Several unrelated, boxed-off item ads that run together on one page of a newspaper to secure a better position than items would get if run alone.

Busy As in "This ad looks too busy," meaning there's too much going on in the ad. Also used by buyers in describing an ad they don't like but aren't quite sure why.

Buyers The store's line officers. Officially they plan their department merchandise to make a profit, buy the merchandise, supervise salespeople and behind-the-scene service personnel, and may even sell to important customers. Unofficially, they rewrite ads, re-do (by instruction) art, and revamp displays. They are indefatigable travelers (to market). Buyers report to divisional merchandise managers.

Buying Office A New York organization (some stores also have buying offices on the West Coast and in Europe and Asia) that conducts the store's buying of merchandise (or advises on buying) when the store's buyers aren't in New York.

Catalog Showroom Store An operation that displays merchandise, offers catalog. Merchandise may be picked out and taken home by the customer.

Charge Accounts The store's lifeblood, credit. Almost every store has them now, even many discounters do. There are three basic kinds: (1) Regular account, which requires that the bill is paid in full every 30 days; (2) Permanent budget, which requires the customer to pay a set amount monthly plus carrying charges; and (3) Credit account (formerly time payment)—so much down, so much a month until merchandise is paid off, with carrying charges added each month. Many stores now have added American Express and bank credit cards like Bankamericard and Master Charge to their own credit plans for even more customer convenience.

Charge Back The bill that a store issues to manufacturers to collect money owed them for co-op or vendor-paid ads.

Christmas Season Begins as soon after Labor Day as a retailer dares—ordinarily after Thanksgiving. Most stores do at least 25 percent of their yearly business in the Christmas season, some more.

Circular Sometimes called a tabloid. A newspaper insert or occupant mailer of store specials.

Comparison Shopper Not a customer, though many customers perform this function for themselves. A store employee who shops the competition for price and quality comparison and to discover the competition's hot items. Comparison shoppers' reports are useful in fending off the BBB, sometimes even the FTC.

Competition Any other retailer who's beating the store out of a sale. Department stores (perhaps unrealistically) feel that they only compete with other department stores, but they have been known to meet a discounter's lower price, or a specialty store's services.

196

Co-op A prerequisite for most ads to run. See **vendor money**.

Copy The text of an ad used by a copywriter to sell a piece of merchandise, store image, or services. Copy consists of a headline, a copy block (selling words to incite customer action), a price, and a floor line. The size of the price indicates the importance of the sale and/or the kind of store that's running the ad. See **schlock**.

Courtesy Days Not the days you can expect to be well treated by the salespeople, which should be every day. Courtesy days are the first days of a sale when charge or special list customers are invited to shop ahead of the rush. Also called a private sale.

Customer The single most valuable unit in retailing.

Cut A copper or steel photograhic engraving made by an acid etching process from a piece of artwork. A newspaper picture may be produced from the "cut" or a mat can be rolled for more than one reproduction.

Discontinued An item a manufacturer wants to unload for one reason or another and offers to retailers at a special price.

Discounter The traditional store's biggest competitor and bugaboo. Objective definition: a low-overhead, mass merchandiser, generally self-service with extended store hours and few customer services. It usually operates on lower mark-up than a traditional department store.

Display Department The part of a store's sales-promotion division that plans and executes in-store and window promotion of merchandise. The sign shop where merchandise signs are made is part of "display." The display manager usually reports to the store sales-promotion manager.

Divisional Merchandise Manager (Also called Divisional) Heads up a division (below).

Divisions (Merchandise) Large related groups of departments headed by a divisional merchandise manager. Here is a typical breakdown from a nationwide store group:

Soft Lines		Hard Lines	
Div. 1	Men's and boys' wear.	Div. 1	Home furnishings: linen, furniture, housewares, gifts.
Div. 2	Ready-to-wear.		
Div. 3	Children's wear, intimate apparel.	Div. 2	Major appliances, rugs.

Div. 4   Fashion accessories
and small-wares
(main-floor
merchandise).

Some stores have a separate division for basement merchandise and others merchandise vertically with the upstairs men's buyer buying downstairs merchandise, too.

Dog Merchandise that doesn't sell. Also called mark-downs.

Domestics Sheets, blankets, pillows, comforters, pillowcases.

Downstairs Store Bargain basement. Though some downstairs stores aren't budget departments (they're furniture or housewares departments), when they have merchandise other than budget goods they're called something else. "Downstairs store" invariably means bargain basement.

Downtown The central business district where most stores are located. Also called the "flagship store" among the suburban branches.

Dumb Coat Not necessarily a bad-looking coat for women, though not a brand-new fashion look either. A basic that a certain number of customers will want to buy year after year.

EDP Electronic Data Processing. Computerized information on inventory, open to buy, personnel, charge accounts—any store function the store puts into the computer bank for later retrieval.

Event A special promotion of an off-price nature, a storewide sale or merchanidse fair.

Exclusive "We're the only place in town you can get this." Also called "confined lines," "our own," and "ours alone." Not only used for national brands, but also store's own label created to compete with national brands and other stores' exclusives.

Eyeball Control Old-fashioned unit control system, dear to the hearts of older buyers. A glance around the floor would presumably reveal what was selling, what to reorder, and what to mark down. Modern stores have replaced eyeball control with EDP.

Fashion Coordinator The arbiter of taste between the merchants and advertising staffs. Goes on buying trips to spot trends and see that the store is following them, interprets trends back at the store. Fashion has become so rampant today that every division probably has a fashion coordinator.

198

Fashion Seasons These have nothing to do with the seasons of the calendar. Fall fashion promotion starts in July and some stores start promoting resort clothes after Thanksgiving.

FTC Federal Trade Commission. A government regulatory body created to protect fair competition in the United States. The FTC takes special interest in cooperative advertising and issues periodic "Guidelines" outlining what is considered a restraint of trade and consequently illegal. It also polices advertising claims.

Figures The gross a department, division, or total store earns in a given time period. Always placed side by side with last year's figures, for purposes of comparison. Figures (usually last year's) determine ad budgets, open-to-buy, and a merchant's day-to-day disposition.

Floor Department selling space. "It's on the floor," means it's on the selling floor.

Floor Line The location of a department by floor, given below the copy block in an ad or at end of a radio commercial.

Floor Manager The woman or man wearing the white or red carnation who is the floor maitre d'. Floor supervisors solve customer problems: okaying returns, taking complaints, helping salespeople write up sales, giving directions.

Ford A hot item that sells consistently. Fords used to be clothes but there are now home-furnishing and gift Fords.

Foreign Office A store or group of stores' resident buying office outside the United States.

Full Line A store with both hard- and soft-line merchandise. All merchandise divisions stocked.

Furniture Warehouse Store High-velocity furniture retailer where furniture is selected from a warehouse. Taken home by customer.

General Merchandise Manager (GMM) VP and VIP, ordinarily the store's No. 3 position after the Chairman of the Board and the President. Divisional merchandise managers report to the GMM and he or she is responsible for the overall direction of the store: merchandise, policy, and sales promotion.

Gift Certificate A voucher for merchandise sold to shoppers who can't decide what special gift to select. Usually redeemable only in "store money" rather than cash.

Hang-Tags or Tickets These are attached to merchandise and tell price, style, department, and season numbers. Some hang-tags now activate alarms to alert personnel to possible shoplifting.

Hard Lines Home furnishings, toys, sporting goods, and appliances, plus some seemingly "soft" hard lines which include curtains, linens, bedspreads, and the like.

Hot Item Merchandise that a buyer really believes in. See **item**.

Image The store's personality, usually from the point of view of store executives rather than the store's customers, though most stores have on-going programs to change, enhance, or better the image they feel they have in the community.

Import Fair Special promotion of merchandise from one or more foreign countries that features regular price imports, visits by the country's celebrities and dignitaries, and tie-ins with tourist offices and airlines.

In the Market A buyer's visit to a manufacturer. If it's a New York buyer, he or she is on Seventh Avenue or in Europe; if an out-of-town buyer, he or she is in New York or sometimes in Chicago (housewares, gifts) or California (sportswear).

Inventory Book inventory is a written (or computerized) record of what there is to sell. If written, the inventory is determined by a unit control person who adds merchandise on-hand at the beginning of the period to merchandise received and subtracts merchandise sold (by counting the stubs of hang-tags). Physical inventory, a check on "book inventory," is an actual count of merchandise taken twice a year. The difference between the book and physical inventory is called overage or shrinkage, an increasing concern of stores everywhere.

Island A table or other store fixture in the middle of the floor where specials are displayed.

Item An individual piece of merchandise, frequently something hot, that a buyer believes in strongly, stocks in many colors and sizes, and runs ads on.

Item Advertising In newspapers, a single piece of merchandise in an ad of its own. In radio, two items are often combined in a 60-second commercial.

Kill To declare an ad "dead" or not running because of nonarrival of merchandise, lower competitive prices, executive mandate.

Knock-Off The lifeblood of fashion retailing (both men's and women's)—making a cheaper copy of a fashion. During any season many fashions are killed by "knock-offs" which cheapen the original in the minds of its buyers. A perfect example is a gold Cartier love bracelet that sold for $250 this season and was knocked off by Revlon for $4 in a cheaper metal.

Layaway A deferred payment system (not as popular in these days of universal credit cards) where customers put a deposit on merchandise they want and come back later to pay the balance.

Layout A plan for a newspaper ad done in pencil or ink and usually reproduced in quantity so merchandisers, buyers, artists, typesetters, and copywriters can all have their own copy. Layouts indicate headlines, copy blocks, and art areas.

Linage Space a newspaper ad runs in. Space in most papers is measured in actual inches deep multiplied by the number of columns wide. 4" x 3 columns is a 12" ad. Large city papers measure space in lines of which there are 14 in an inch. Thus a 12" ad contains 168 lines. A full page is 2400 lines in a full-size paper, 1000 lines in a tabloid size.

Line Many store meanings, including: (1) all the merchandise shown by one manufacturer or designed in one season; (2) newspaper space (explained under linage).

Lines The whole store inventory, as in "full-line store."

Logo A store's or manufacturer's signature, also called a sig cut, which identifies the store's advertising quickly. Many stores resist using a manufacturer's "logo" in their ads, even when the manufacturer invests heavily in cooperative advertising.

Loss Leader An item advertised at an exceptionally low price to bring customers in or create traffic. Frequently used to trade up to a better item in same merchandise category.

Mark-Downs Unsold merchandise is "marked down" periodically until sold. Many stores' "mark-down" policies require a certain percentage of price reduction at each mark-down. Such merchandise is sometimes the result of buyers' mistakes. Buyers prefer to regard it as merchandise that was ahead of the customers' taste.

Mark-On or Mark-Up Used interchangeably in retailing, meaning the difference between the cost price of merchandise and the retail price. "Mark-on" or "mark-up" covers operating expenses (salaries, overhead, promotion) and a reasonable profit. NRMA figures cumulative department-store average mark-up at 43.9 percent. Mark-up may also be used as a verb when discussing how much merchandise has been "marked up."

Mat A piece of asbestos cardboard molded around a cut to reproduce (not quite as sharply as the cut would) a picture for a newspaper ad. Mats are used by smaller stores that don't use artists. These stores buy a "mat service" or catalog of stock pictures available on mats to use instead of artwork. Because of the technical process of newspaper printing, mats reproduce smaller than original size. This is known as "mat shrinkage."

Merchandise What a store has to sell, also called stock.

Night Openings The night(s) stores are open. More stores stay open more nights every year to capture more business from competition.

NRMA National Retail Merchants' Association, department stores' and specialty stores' trade association which provides management, merchandising, and sales-promotion guidance to members.

Off-Price A promotional price. The reasons for merchandise being "off-price" include special purchases for a sale, slight irregularities (which will not mar the beauty or durability), sample sizes or showroom samples, a promotional buy, discontinued styles, and end-of-season clearances.

On the Floor Said of those in a store who can't be found in their accustomed place. Possibly they are selling, supervising, in advertising, taking a coffee break, or gone for the day.

Open to Buy The amount of money a buyer is allotted to spend in a given period to keep stocks at a healthy, better-than-last-year level.

Order Board A switchboard (often a special one) that receives phone orders placed by customers. Frequently, the "order board" stays open when the store is closed.

Outpost A branch of a department in another part of the same store. Frequently "outposts" stock merchandise from several departments to help customers put fashion items together.

Over-Bought The condition of a buyer who has too much merchandise and no open-to-buy.

Personal Shopper A store employee who does the shopping for customers to their exacting specifications.

Pick-up Ads that run in the downtown store and are later "picked-up" and rerun by branch stores or rerun by the main store. "Pick-ups" lower the overall ad cost by eliminating new copy and art.

Pieces The quantity of any item a buyer has on hand. Many stores require that there be a certain number of "pieces" on hand before an ad runs.

Profit What's left for the stockholders when everyone has gotten his or her share. NRMA figures the average net department-store profit after taxes was 3.08 percent last year.

Promotion (1) An event to sell merchandise, generally specially priced. Promotions are ways to generate store traffic. (2) Something a buyer purchases to promote, for example, a group of off-priced suits.

Promotion Plan A written outline of the sales objectives of a department (or a division or store) for any given period, and how the buyer intends to accomplish them. A six months' plan is made by the buyer, then okayed and modified by the merchandise manager. Generally the plan is made concrete 30 days ahead of the given month and is called the monthly plan. "Promotion plans" are based on previous year's sales plus a percent of the increase (or decrease) the department is currently showing.

Promotional Said of stores that run a lot of off-price ads and are sharp about pricing regular merchandise, too. "Promotional" stores frequently run borax ads.

Proof An impression of a print ad submitted by the newspaper or magazine to the advertiser for approval in advance of publication. A proof contains copy set in type, impressions of artwork, engravings, and the store's logo within the space the ad will run. The advertising department checks proof with buyers, corrects inaccuracies and positioning, and sends it back to the paper with a release (final okay) or request for a second "proof."

Protection The store detectives. Shoplifters—a growing problem for retailers—must be pursued and arrested outside the store in New York and many other states. Otherwise (the law says) they might intend to return the merchandise to stock.

Put a Bell On A method of finding important store executives who are on the floor. When his or her autobell number rings throughout the store, the executive picks up a phone and gets the message or call that's waiting.

Rag Merchants Soft-line retailers who sell schlock merchandise. Most of them are earnestly trying to trade up.

Receiving Where merchandise comes into a store. The "receiving" dock is the street unloading point. The dock sends merchandise to the "receiving" room where it is ticketed with all the information by the department.

Release	The final okay slip on a print-ad proof that says in effect that the advertising department takes full responsibility for any inaccuracies undetected in the proof . . . unless they occur when the proof gets back to the paper.
Resource	Vendor/manufacturer. Sometimes the object of keen competition by different buyers in same store if it's a good and with-it manufacturer, that is, a maker of wanted items.
Returns	What doesn't stay sold . . . the bane of a buyer's (customer returns) or manufacturer's (buyer returns) existence. A store's "return" policy (whether it's liberal or sticky) as well as its credit policy are both useful in determining its profit picture and personality.
Runner	An item that "doesn't do anything but sell," a phrase that's right up there with "you can't argue with success" in buyers' truisms.
Sales Promotion	A store division with responsibility for selling the store and store merchandise. Responsibilities include broadcast, newspaper, direct mail, display, signing, and publicity. Some "sales-promotion" departments are also in charge of salespeople's merchandise training.
Schlock	Used to describe low quality, cheap merchandise being sold by competition. Also the store where "schlock" merchandise is sold.
Season Letter	Not connected with Christmas correspondence. Coded alphabet letters on price tickets to tell the buyer (but not the customers) when stock came into the store or how old it is.
Service Desk	Where a customer goes to return merchandise, complain, pick up shopping bags, and have purchases wrapped.
Services	Extras offered by stores to make shopping there a pleasanter experience. Typical services are free parking, snack and restaurant facilities, gift wrap, delivery, post office, night opening (though this may be as much of a service to a store as it is to the customers). Discount stores have fewer services than department stores because they operate at a lower mark-up.
Shop	Also called the shop concept. A special selling area organized around seasons (ski or swimsuit shops), or category selectivity (putting together everything a certain kind of customer might want: gifts, garden supplies, new fashions with accessories) or designers' own shops, the newest shop concept.
Shrinkage	Merchandise that disappears through carelessness, shoplifting, etc., from one inventory to the next. A high shrinkage percentage is grounds for buyer dismissal.

Sizes, Definitions of Junior sizes 3 to 13, (sometimes up to 15) fit smaller, higher-waisted figures in styles that are younger looking; Jr. Petite sizes 3 to 11 for even smaller and shorter Junior figures. Misses (most likely figure type), for sizes 4 to 14 (though you can technically have a misses' fashion up to size 18, not many department stores stock these sizes, they're mostly available at special-size stores). Half-sizes for ampler, shorter-waisted figures are 14½ to 26½ and are also called "custom sizes." Women's sizes are another range for larger figures and run from 38 to 46, sometimes up to 52. Men's sizes have traditionally been less varied with suits coming in short, medium, tall, and extra tall lengths and chest sizes; shirts in neck and sleeve sizes, and pants in waist and inseam sizes. Now there's a tendency for men's wear to come in more big-and-tall sizes. There's some tendency in both women's and men's sizes toward simplification to small, medium, and large.

Soft Lines All merchandise that is not home furnishings, toys, sporting goods, appliances, or TBA.

Specialty Shop A retail store that concentrates on men's, women's, or children's fashion or one sex group (men's or women's) or age group (babies) or activity (skiing) or collectors' items (antiques). Opposite of a full-line store.

Spot In newspaper advertising, a small subillustration which differs from a bug in that it shows additional uses for the advertised merchandise. For instance, the main picture would show an ensemble with the jacket on, the "spot" would show the dress alone.

Store Hours The hours a store stays open. The trend is toward Monday- and Thursday-night openings downtown and every-night openings in the suburbs.

Store Money The customer gets "store money" two ways, as change from a gift certificate and by returning something not credited to his or her charge account or cash refunded. Stores prefer to keep the money in the store, of course.

Stuffer The ads that are put in customers' monthly bills from stores. Usually all are vendor-paid or co-opped.

Success As in "you can't argue with success," a succinct argument for doing things the way the store has always done them.

Suggestion Selling Example: "How about a Polo shirt to go with the Cardin blazer, sir?" The salesperson pulling off this coup can be considered an expert at "suggestion selling."

Sunday Openings Many stores first tested these during the Christmas season a couple of years ago, discovered additional revenue, and extended open Sundays year round. Many people have reservations.

Systems Store "systems" are all the things a store salesperson has to learn in order to sell, and they're considerable: how to register a sale, how to write a charge, C.O.D., will call, layaway sales, how to make an exchange, suggestion selling, and trading-up, to mention only a few.

Take-withs Purchases the customer carries home. These are very popular with stores because of soaring delivery costs.

Tear Sheet An ad taken from the publication in which it ran. This is used as proof positive that ad ran on the page and day it was supposed to and is evidence for collecting co-op money.

Tie-in An ad sponsored by more than one advertiser as a magazine spread in which a store, airline, and luggage manufacturer participate. A tie-in might also feature a store's import fair and a European tourist bureau in a newspaper or radio.

Toppers Signs put on top of display cards signaling something of special interest: "As Advertised on Radio," or "Anniversary Special."

Trading up Selling customers something more expensive than they came in to buy. Always important when loss leaders are advertised. Trading up is a more civilized form of bait and switch.

Traffic The ebb and flow of people into a store. May be motivated by ads or rain, a good store location, or rest-room facilities, but the general rule remains: the more people milling about, the more sales.

Training Squad College graduates, usually, being trained for a year or so as store's future executives. Today's trainees represent the new breed of figures executives as opposed to yesterday's instinctive retailers.

Transaction What one customer buys from one salesperson on one visit to a store. An individual sale.

Turnover Also called turn. The velocity with which merchandise passes from merchant to customer and new merchandise is ordered. The faster the "turn over," the brisker the business, though not necessarily the better the business. Discounters turn merchandise about twice as fast as the average department store—approximately seven turns a year.

Twig A small branch store, usually under $5 million volume, not carrying the full line.

Unit Control The organization responsible for book inventory. The stubs pulled when merchandise is sold are counted and subtracted from the number of pieces on-hand in the unit control book so the buyer can tell what's selling and what needs reordering.

UPS United Parcel Service, a private nationwide delivery service for stores. Most stores use UPS though some do their own delivery. UPS also delivers mail in most cities in the United States.

Vendor Money Also called co-op. The co-operative money available from manufacturers to share the cost of running an ad. Most stores count on getting a sizable portion of their ad budget from their vendors, some even make money on co-op advertising.

Vendors Manufacturers or suppliers.

Volume The gross business a store does in a year. The difference between "volume" and cost of doing business is profit.

White Goods (1) Linens for bed, bath, and table. "White goods" generally go on sale at least three times a year: January, May, and August. (2) Only in the trade: major appliances like refrigerators and stoves. Brown goods are radios and TVs.

White Space The part of a newspaper ad that's left after art, copy, logo, store hours, and other services are put in.

Will-Call Merchandise that will be picked up later either because it's being altered or being paid for. A layaway is one kind of "will-call."

Window "I've got a window" doesn't mean that a buyer is high in the firm and has a good office. Buyers' offices are mostly in undesirable stockrooms under the racks. Having a window means a display of merchandise in a store window. This is another way of building that all-important store traffic.

Wanted Also **most wanted**, a favorite buyer phrase for headlines; e.g., this year's most "wanted" styles and colors. Very often a dodge when the buyer isn't sure what styles and colors will be in the shipment.

Winner See **runner, action item.**

Women's Wear Daily Trade paper of department stores and soft-line merchants published by Fairchild Publications. Other Fairchild papers cater to other merchandisers: *Home Furnishings Daily* for hard lines and *Daily News Record* for men's wear retailers.

DATE DUE

JAN 29 '85		
FB 22 '85		
MAY 7 '85		
OCT 4 '85		
AP 25 '86		
DEC 04 '87		
AP 15 '88		
DE 2 '90		
DE 20 '91		
DF 04 '92		